Confronting Betrayals and
Reclaiming My Self-Worth

I CALL
BULLSHIT

Becca Christensen

Ignite Publishing
Austin, Texas
www.thebeccachristensen.com
info@thebeccachristensen.com

Hardback: 979-8-9895105-0-4
Paperback: 979-8-9895105-1-1
eBook: 979-8-9895105-2-8

Cover and interior design by Jess LaGreca, Mayfly Design

Library of Congress Catalog Number: 2023921709

First Printing: 2024
Printed in United States of America

CONTENTS

Author's Note   vii

Blindsided   1
Trapped   11
Stand By My Man   25
Quiet Defiance   31
Devastated and Confused   39
Snapped   57
Something New   67
Compromise   75
Enough Is Enough   89
Too Little, Too Late   97
Truth and Tornadoes   109
One Step at a Time   123
Defiant Hope   135
Will the True Me Please Stand Up?   145
Reigniting the Spark Within   155
She Was There the Whole Time   167
Epilogue   177

Acknowledgments   185

AUTHOR'S NOTE

This book is a reflection of my truth—what I saw, felt, and experienced during an especially challenging time in my life. Memory is an intense and intriguing world to dive into—and that's particularly true when it comes to memories centered around trauma. The stories and dialogue in this memoir are told as honestly and faithfully as I can recall and are true to what I believe happened. I have changed some names and descriptions, and I have reconstructed dialogue to the best of my recollection. Others who were present might recall things differently. But this is my story.

Some scenes and situations may be uncomfortable to read. Believe me, they were uncomfortable to experience. While I would like to kindly make note of the potential discomfort in reading some of these memories, I would also encourage you to acknowledge that discomfort when it arises, sit with it, and see what it's bringing up within you. Perhaps by reading my story, you will uncover more depth within yourself and find connection to others.

My life experiences, struggles, and betrayals are certainly not the worst ever experienced by a human, and I am not here to be a victim, for you to feel sorry for me, or for us to wallow in a vat of self-pity. I want us, as a collective humanity, to stop comparing our lives, struggles, and traumas. We all have them. Let's instead acknowledge that everyone has their shit and there is not a better or worse, there just . . . is. Let's hold space and support each other as we travel on this lifelong journey toward knowing ourselves and our worth. This is a continuous journey, one that requires action, presence, grace, patience, and love. The path involves complex movements backward, inward, outward, forward, sideways—and perhaps a funky dance move every now and then.

It is beyond humbling to imagine you reading this book. I have pictured it, dreamed it, and now it's actually happening! It's both terrifying and wonderful. My deepest hope is that my story, my words, ring true to you. Even if our life experiences have been vastly different, there is a connection that can be formed from our compassion for each other. We are not alone.

BLINDSIDED

FEBRUARY 2009

O ur house was mostly dark, but the light over the dining room table illuminated my recent project—making a scrapbook of the Disney World vacation my husband, Jason, and I had taken that past Christmas. We'd been back for about a month, and I had just started organizing all the photos from our trip. The table was covered with pictures and a warm, fuzzy feeling rose inside me as I looked at them. I picked up my favorite, taken on Christmas Eve.

It was a selfie of me and Jason, huddled together in the center of the park, another loving couple amid thousands, waiting in anticipation for the holiday celebration to begin. As the lights dimmed, the carols grew louder, and then, suddenly, fireworks burst into the sky, raining fairy dust over Cinderella's enchanted castle. I was wrapped in Jason's arms, mesmerized by the beauty. I leaned my head back against his chest and the love that I felt for him and he for me flowed between us. As the final fireworks shimmered above, I turned around and we shared a magical kiss.

I smiled to myself as I set the photo back down. Disney might be the last vacation we took just the two of us. Next month, I was going to stop taking birth control and we were going to start trying for a baby. I was twenty-four, and I felt ready to have a family.

I had completed my teaching degree and graduated right before we left for Disney World. The school where I completed my internship had offered me a full-time job, which meant that I would be able to keep working with people I adored. A few of them were much older than me and felt like parental figures. They were so kind, and they offered me the encouragement, support, and easy friendship I'd longed for. I'd only started my internship there in the fall, but I already felt like I was part of the team and loved my job.

I stepped into the kitchen to finish cleaning up from dinner, feeling light and happy. Those Disney pictures were evidence that I was living the life I had always dreamed of. Things were good with Jason, college was done, I was starting my career, my new teaching position was awesome, and I loved our new house. What we had created was drastically different and so much better than what I had experienced as a kid. I couldn't really explain it, but I felt a strange undercurrent of hope, mixed with satisfaction and contentment. It felt like Jason and I were entering into a new chapter of our lives, but at the same time, I knew that all of this was already everything I'd wished for.

I tossed our paper plates in the garbage and wiped down the counter. We usually had fast-food or take-out for dinner, since that was easy and what Jason preferred, but tonight I had made one of Jason's favorite meals—chili cheese dogs. Growing up, I hadn't really learned how to cook, so experimenting with cooking often meant mistakes or failure, neither of which I was very interested in. But who can mess up chili cheese dogs? Warm up the buns, hot dogs, and a can of chili, spread the chili over the hot dogs and buns, and top it all with cheese. Done. No risk, no creativity, no thought, but it meant a happy husband and easy cleanup.

As I finished in the kitchen, I realized I could still hear ESPN blabbing in the background. Watching TV was Jason's favorite way to relax after his long day managing a restaurant, so we often had the sports channel on while we sat on the couch and ate dinner. But now that he was in the shower, I didn't need to hear, for the fiftieth time, all the reasons why one team had won and another team had lost. I took a final look at the kitchen, dried my hands, and turned off the TV. The room was gloriously silent for just a second before Jason's cell phone rang.

Jason was the only restaurant manager at our local Italian eatery and often received emergency calls when he was off duty. Having worked in restaurants myself, I knew the business could be unpredictable. Since he was in the shower, I decided to answer his phone in case it was anything urgent. I felt a little zing of satisfaction and pride, knowing that I was being kind and helpful. Having been married for only nine months, we still felt like newlyweds, and I believed that being a good wife meant supporting my husband in his career. I picked up his phone from the coffee table and headed toward our bedroom, prepared to interrupt Jason's shower if necessary.

"Hello?" I said, as I flipped open the phone and entered our bedroom.

"Hello," came an irritated female voice. "Who is this?"

Taken aback, I responded, with some attitude, "Uh, who is *this*?"

"I need to know who this is," she retorted.

"And I need to know who *this* is," I sassed back.

"I know, but who is this? I'm trying to determine who this is," she repeated.

I laughed sharply. "Well, I don't know this number, so who are *you?*"

In the silence that followed, I thought maybe this was one of those relentless telemarketers attempting to con me into giving away personal information over the phone. Or maybe it was some prank call from one of my husband's employees. I rolled my eyes and waited for her to say something else.

"Just tell me who this is," she tried again.

"No! You called this number, so you tell me who you are," I repeated, feeling utterly confused about what the hell was going on.

She sighed, then began to speak in a firm, neutral voice.

"I'm calling from my daughter's phone. I've been seeing messages going back and forth between this number and my daughter's number. I want to make sure that she's okay, so I'm . . . I'm looking into it."

"I'm sorry, what?" I froze, except for my mind, which started to spin.

"I just need to know who this number belongs to," she pleaded.

"I . . . I . . ." I was searching for words to cut through my confusion. Now I really didn't understand what was going on. I stood staring at our bathroom door, which was slightly open. I could hear the water from the shower, and I knew Jason was in there, oblivious to what was happening.

The caller spoke again, this time even more emphatically. "Like I said, the person with this number has been texting my teenage daughter . . . *inappropriate messages* . . . and I need to know who it is."

4

"Well, this isn't *my* phone—" I started to say, not really knowing *what* to say.

A moment passed, and then the woman's voice changed. Sounding stunned, she whispered, "Is this *Becca*?"

My breath caught. What. The. Fuck. Whoever this was knew me, knew my name.

"Yes, this is Becca," I admitted, figuring there was no reason to deny it.

"Becca," she said, "it's Stephanie."

"Stephanie who?!" I blurted out, not thinking.

Then, in a flash, I recognized her voice.

Holy. Shit.

I recognized Stephanie's voice because I had worked with her for six months now. The caller wasn't just the mother of some girl Jason was supposedly texting; she was my coworker, a fellow elementary teacher. And not just a fellow teacher, but literally the teacher in the classroom next door to mine. A woman who I respected and looked up to. A woman I saw and talked to every single day.

"Oh my god, Stephanie." I nearly dropped the phone as I slumped to the floor, squatting at the foot of our bed. I closed my eyes and spoke the truth we both already knew. "This is Jason's phone," I whispered, feeling the world collapsing around me.

Sounding gentler now, Stephanie explained what she had been trying to say before, relating the texts she'd allegedly seen between Jason, my thirty-four-year-old husband, and her sixteen-year-old daughter. I sank onto my butt and held my head in my hands, struggling to make sense of this conversation and keep my mind from exploding.

Stephanie's words came in fits and spurts—inappropriate, relationship, intimate, Jason possibly taking advantage of her daughter, sneaking around. As a mother, she felt worried and wanted answers. I could tell that she was tiptoeing around what she was trying to say, knowing that this information would be hurtful and devastating, no matter what. I felt the weight of each word as it fell, like ten thousand pounds crushing me. The word that I heard loud and clear, although she did not say it, was *sex*.

————

Jason was still in the shower when I ended the phone call. I thought back to Disney World and all those pictures on our table. I had believed that I was Jason's whole world. I knew that he loved me and cared about me, and thought I was beautiful and sexy. I had felt loved and cherished and safe. We had been together for five years before getting married last summer. And now, here's Stephanie, my coworker, alleging that he is cheating on me.

What the hell?

I thought we were happy. Sure, we'd had our ups and downs, but I figured that was normal for a married couple. I understood that restaurant life could be challenging, and Jason had to work long hours. But now, I find out that he's been ~~texting~~ *sexting* a teenager? Given that the girl in question *worked* for Jason, the fact that he'd been spending so much time away from home suddenly seemed suspicious.

I felt angry, pissed that this was a conversation I now had to have with him. I should not be getting random phone calls from someone informing me about my husband's alleged inappropriate behavior.

Of course, I jumped to the worst conclusion—that he was having an affair with this girl, cheating on me. But as the initial shock began to ease, part of me also felt mad and frustrated at

Stephanie—that she would have the balls to call our house, to try to ruin my life like this. Her allegations were vile, disgusting, impossible. While I knew that she had tried to be gentle, her words now felt like missiles fired, carelessly, without any regard to the damage she was causing in the process. In one five-minute call, she had dumped a massive pile of shit at my feet, and now I had to figure out how to clean it up.

As I waited for Jason to finish his shower, I started shaking; my brain was racing a million miles a minute. Because of that stupid call, my life suddenly felt so fragile. After fighting to escape my father's manipulative and abusive behaviors, I'd met Jason and finally built a normal life, a beautiful life. Jason was a good man who knew what I'd been through and had supported me as I severed all ties with my father. Jason had been my only source of love and happiness during those challenging years. He was my rock, my safe place. This life we had created together was my *everything*.

Stephanie's words kept ricocheting around my mind. I couldn't stop thinking of all the things that could possibly be going on and wondering how in the hell Jason was going to explain this. I had his phone in my hand; I could have checked his text messages right then and there to confirm what Stephanie had said. But this was 2009—it wasn't so easy to scroll through texts. And, honestly? I was so angry that it didn't even occur to me. Just the possibility that someone I loved—who claimed they loved me—was being disloyal and unfaithful to me was unimaginable. Was our whole marriage a lie? If what Stephanie was saying was true, then had my whole relationship with Jason been one lie after another?

I could sense my life unraveling. My body was burning up, turning inside out; I felt uneven and confused and hot. I heard the water shut off, and when Jason walked into our bedroom a few minutes later with a towel wrapped around his waist, my anger was unleashed.

"I just got a call on your phone from Stephanie. She's saying that there are messages between your number and her daughter's! Are you cheating on me? Have you been with another girl? Stephanie is trying to figure out what's happening and *I* need to know what the fuck is going on!"

Jason took in this information, looking only mildly surprised. When my rant ended, he calmly denied everything. "No," he started, "that's not what's happening." He put his hands on my shoulders and looked into my eyes. "Becca, her daughter is just an emotional teenager. Stephanie is exaggerating and she's making something out of nothing." I looked away from him, still hearing Stephanie's voice in my head.

"But, what did you do?" I asked, angrily. "Why would she be saying this? Why would she have texts?"

He began rubbing my arms lightly. "You know how it is, Becca . . . we have to text for work, to figure out the employee schedule and stuff, but that's it. There's nothing going on. Her daughter is just a silly girl trying to get attention."

All of the emotions colliding inside of me as I listened to Jason speak made my brain feel fuzzy. I had been so angry just seconds ago, but now his voice was dulling that rage into confusion. I didn't know if I believed him or not. He was the manager; of course, he would text his employees. As for the girl, my perception of her was that she was an immature teenager. I had seen her with her boyfriends at the restaurant and at company barbecues before. But she knew me! She knew that Jason was married, and that I was his wife. Why would she do this to us? Maybe she *was* imagining there was something more with Jason. Maybe she *was* just trying to get attention. Jason was the one who really knew what was going on, so why would I second-guess him?

"Becca," he said, pulling me to him, "I don't know what you're so upset about. I don't like her. I love *you*." I watched his tempting lips say the words I needed to hear. I looked up into his dark brown, almost black, eyes and melted into him.

Jason was my partner. He was my best friend and the only man I had ever loved. I'd known him longer than I had known Stephanie, and I trusted him with my heart and soul. I had to trust him about this; the alternative seemed impossible. If the tables were turned, I would want him to trust me. I would *expect* him to trust me. We were married, for crying out loud. Jason had been loyal and honest with me the whole time we'd been together, and he had never given me any reason to doubt him. I didn't know why Stephanie's daughter would try to ruin him like this, but I was going to remain fiercely loyal to my husband. In my mind, there simply wasn't any other option.

He put his arms around me and held me close, then pulled me down to sit on the bed next to him. "I love you, Becca. You are the only one for me." He smiled, then shook his head. "This is nothing. Don't worry about it."

We talked for a while. Him, nearly naked; me, vulnerable and emotional. I started to cry again, feeling relieved and reassured, the call now starting to feel like maybe it had just been a bad dream. He wiped my tears away and kissed me, easing me back on the bed as the towel slipped from his waist. He covered my body with his and the familiar weight of him made me feel safe and loved. Whatever had happened, it wasn't the worst. He was telling me the truth.

TRAPPED

1993

"Becca, tell me the truth. Did he touch you?" my mom asked, holding me at arm's length as my eight-year-old body shook. She looked intently into my wide eyes while my baby brother napped on the couch nearby.

"I . . . I don't know what you mean. We were wrestling, and I got scared," I mumbled, confused by her question. She drew me in close and hugged me tight, smoothing my hair.

My six-year-old little sister, Beth, and I had been playing a wrestling game with our dad. My dad got down on all fours and we climbed on him, tugging at his neck, pushing him around, and trying to "pin" him on his back. Most of the time, we loved this game because my dad's attention was fully focused on us. Sometimes, though, he grabbed us and threw us down or pinned us under his own body weight, while we demanded release. Or he would put me in a choke hold where I couldn't breathe, and he wouldn't let me go right away. I hated the feeling of being completely overpowered, my face smashed against him, panic rising up against the grip on my throat. This time, I had accidentally kneed him in the eye trying to escape, and the game ended when I ran upstairs, upset.

My mom occasionally spoke up when she saw him getting too rough, dragging out his one-syllable name. "*Ron . . .*" she would caution sternly, leaning against the doorway to the living room, cradling my brother to her chest. My dad might briefly glance at her, then continue to grapple with us.

"What?" he would respond, the annoyance clear in his voice. "We're just playing. They like it." He didn't raise his voice, but his tone implied that my mom was being ridiculous and that it was none of her business how he played with his daughters. Rebuked, she shrank back into the kitchen.

In some ways, my dad was right. When the game was fun, my sister and I giggled and squealed like crazy. We *did* like it—until we didn't. I think my mom understood that the line between okay and not-okay could be crossed too quickly and easily, and she was trying to warn my dad (or maybe us?) before things got out of hand.

My dad never listened to my mom, or any of us, really, because he never thought he did anything wrong. Anytime my mom contradicted him, he discredited her or said something to make her look stupid. When she challenged him, he called her crazy and said she was getting "too emotional." If my mom didn't do his bidding or agree with him, whatever the issue, we all had to walk on eggshells for the rest of the night, in fear of his volatile temper.

At church, of course, things were different. There, my dad was all smiles as our family paraded into the sanctuary. He greeted others and shook hands, one hand pressed lovingly (or was it possessively?) to my mom's lower back, as he volunteered for whatever event was coming up next. He didn't seem to care whether the event conflicted with a family activity or, when I got older, with one of my volleyball games. Sitting in the pews, we listened to sermons about the roles and responsibilities of parents, and how children should obey their mom and dad. I somehow got the impression that, by us being in church, my parents were doing what God wanted them to do and that made them good people and "good Christians." My dad certainly played the role of the *good Christian man* to a tee—when others were watching, that is.

If my dad was feeling especially proud of me and wanted to show me off, he would pull me to his side and say, "Aww, my Junior," with a big, glowing smile that unabashedly revealed his crooked teeth. Admittedly, we had the same eyes, the same dark hair color, the same large nose, and, eventually, the same strong, tall build.

Looking back, maybe that was it—maybe our physical similarities confused him and made him think he had the right to take certain liberties with my body and my space, because I practically *was* him, wasn't I? He was good at blurring the lines.

There was no question that I was much closer to my mom, but as I got older, it was harder to get quality time with her. She had to take care of so many other things: juggling my little brother, driving us around, doing laundry, cooking dinner, cleaning the house. After my brother was born, she seemed significantly more exhausted in general. She slept with him when he napped and sometimes longer, until it no longer surprised us to find her asleep at any point during the day. Between all her responsibilities, her naps, and my school schedule, there wasn't much time for us to spend together. I had to make the most of every opportunity. There were even several times when, instead of pausing while my mom went to use the bathroom during one of our conversations, I just followed her in there so we could keep talking. I didn't want to risk losing my chance to be with her.

Our family was always pretty open when it came to using the restroom or bathing. When you're little, you don't get much privacy; that's just a given. I had no qualms about being naked then, laughing and singing my booty off while Beth and I played Barbies and Ninja Turtles in the tub, and my mom sprayed foam beards and hats on us. Because my mom stayed at home with us, we were used to her being around. But even when I was young, I was aware of the difference between boys and girls, and eventually, it started to feel awkward having my dad with me in the bathroom while I was using the toilet. After all, my mom and sister and I all had the same parts, but my dad obviously didn't. When talking to *him*, I always tried to end whatever conversation we were having, and then run to go pee, hoping he wouldn't follow me into the bathroom. With time, I developed into a stealthy spy: I was quick and quiet, changing up my route through the house—down the hallway, duck into the bedroom, out again after he passed, and back down the hall the other way—ultimately using whichever toilet was farthest away from my dad.

When my dad found me, as he often did, he entered the bathroom like a stage manager, flinging open the door without knocking first, with no regard for my privacy. The utter confidence with which he strode through the door seemed like a declaration of his right to be there. His entire demeanor conveyed his belief that his interruption was totally normal and appropriate—necessary or special, even.

"Daaaaad!" I would cry out, as I scrunched up and tried to cover myself.

"Oh Becca," he'd say, dismissing my protests. "I saw you naked as a baby. It's not a big deal. It's normal, you're fine."

But seeing me as a baby was different than seeing me as I became older. My body was changing, and I was fully capable of using the restroom without any help, *thank you very much*. And wasn't it *my* body? Shouldn't *I* be able to decide who saw it? At the same time, I was still young, only eight—how was I to know what was normal and what wasn't? If my dad didn't feel weird about these bathroom visits, why should I?

Even as a growing girl, locking the door never crossed my mind because it simply wasn't allowed, and it never had been. For as long as I could remember, my dad always said, "We don't lock doors in this family. There is no need to keep each other out." Because this message was so deeply ingrained, I felt like locking the door was wrong. My dad implied that you only locked doors if you were hiding something, sneaking around or being naughty. I felt guilty for even wanting to lock the door, as though my desire for privacy meant I was a bad person or being disobedient. I wasn't trying to hide anything! I was doing all I could to be good! But the bottom line was that my dad was the boss of the house, and his rules were our rules. If I locked the door, I would be punished, and I feared what that would look like. Eventually, I started to rebel in other ways I hoped wouldn't get me in trouble. "I'll be right out!" I'd say as I ran into the bathroom, quickly closing the door behind me. "I'll talk to you in a minute!" I'd call out, rushing to wipe and pull up my underwear when I heard his footsteps approaching.

When this happened, my dad ignored me and pushed open the door as usual. "You're being ridiculous, Becca. There's nothing wrong with me being in here with you. We're family." He never averted his gaze or shielded his eyes as I sat there,

embarrassed and hunched over, with my clothing tucked between my knees.

The obvious message was that he had a right to be in that
space whenever and however he wanted, no matter who else
was in there or what they were doing. He *belonged* in the bathroom with me. It was *his* house and I was *his* daughter.

More than once, I asked him to *please get out* as he stood
there, watching me pee. There I was, sitting on the toilet, already finished doing what I needed to do, and still, he didn't
leave. "Dad, can you please just give me a few minutes? I'll
come talk to you as soon as I'm done."

"Oh, just do what you need to do, Becca. It's fine."

I felt trapped with the toilet paper in hand, ready to wipe
and dress. My mind scrambled to figure out how to politely
argue for my privacy, while my body clenched up, trying to become as small and hidden as possible under my dad's watchful
eyes. This was my good, Christian dad. The man who attended
church with his family three times a week, sometimes more.
Was it natural for him to be in the bathroom with his preteen
daughter while she used the toilet? Was I being unreasonable?
Was I being rude when I asked him to leave? Was I, as he put it,
misinterpreting the situation? Did he have a right to be there?

Even though my dad said his visits were normal, my body's
reactions told me that he was invading my privacy and that his
behavior wasn't okay. Those feelings were just so small and
quiet, though, buried underneath his logic, reasons, and words
which filled my mind. I was truly confused and conflicted, not
fully understanding what was going on. I didn't feel the need
to tell anyone in the beginning, because I didn't know for sure
that what was happening was wrong. There was even a part of
me that thought maybe my dad and I had a special relationship, stronger than others. The way he acted made it seem like

I should be happy about his visits, not upset. That I should see his presence as a privilege.

I hated this tug-of-war inside of me and the constant feeling of not knowing what to do. So, the next time he barged in on me, insisting that his interruption was normal, and I was ridiculous for thinking otherwise, I made a decision: I shoved my intuition deep inside, told my body to be quiet, and ignored the fact that something within me knew that he was wrong.

1997

"Hey, Mom?" I said, slowly pushing open the door to the bedroom where she was folding laundry.

"Hi, honey," she replied kindly. "Come on in. What's up?"

I climbed onto the bed and whispered, "I started my period."

"Again?" she asked, surprised and confused.

Only two weeks had passed since my last one. My mom walked me through the basics when I'd first started earlier that year, but I was only twelve and neither of us was prepared for me to have *two* periods a month. (I assume, now, that this was the first sign of endometriosis and numerous other female issues that have plagued me throughout my life.) The main problem for me, though I didn't say it, was how to deal with my dad. It was bad enough when he came into the bathroom while I was peeing, and I definitely didn't want him in there while I was dealing with blood and pads and tampons and cramps every other week. After I started my period, it soon became obvious that my body was changing in other ways. I grew taller and lankier, developing breasts and exhibiting all those other *glorious* signs of puberty. His bathroom visits no longer seemed as . . . innocent . . . and were more like an experience to be survived. I covered myself as best as I could and vehemently ignored the shame in my belly and the fear in my throat. I needed my body to just chill out and cooperate so I could focus on dealing with the task at hand and with him. It was only a few minutes; I just had to get through them.

I had never told my mom how much I dreaded my dad's bathroom visits—or how often they happened. I didn't know whether or not my mom knew what he was doing and if she thought it was okay. I felt like I wasn't really supposed to talk about it and, anyway, bringing it up now felt like I would just be adding yet another thing for her to deal with. She was taking care of everything else, and I thought it would be most helpful to her if I was as independent and self-sufficient as I could be.

———

As I was taking a shower one evening, I heard my dad say my name. "Hey, Becca. I wanted to ask you something," he said.

Caught off guard, I peeked around the shower curtain and there he was, leaning against the wall, watching me.

"Dad! I'm in the shower! I'm almost done. Can it wait a few minutes?"

As though he hadn't heard me, my dad started talking, telling me about some church event that was happening that weekend. I stayed under the running water longer than I needed to, hoping I could outlast him. Thankfully, he finally left and I quickly jumped out, dried off, and ran to my room before he could come back.

The next week, it happened again, and once or twice a week for years after that. He would slink across the floor until he reached his post against the wall, where the shower curtain provided me little protection from his gaze. I did what I could, painstakingly securing the edges of the shower curtain to the walls, trying to glue them closed with water and suction. But inevitably, they loosened and fell open, allowing him to look at me if he stood in just the right spot. Sometimes, if he couldn't see me, he just pushed the curtain aside himself.

Since the shower was at the far end of the bathroom, there was no escape. I was fully on display with nowhere to hide. No toilet to hunch over or clothes to quickly pull on and cover me up. My towel, on the rack, was just on the other side of him. If I faced the showerhead, I exposed my back and butt to him. If I faced front, I exposed everything else. I stood there, frustrated and annoyed, wondering why I had to choose which direction I faced. Why did I have to worry about what he did or didn't see instead of just being able to wash my hair and clean my body like a normal girl?

I cursed my body, hating that it was something this man— *my dad*—wanted to look at. And I hated the internal battle I was constantly fighting—even though I was trying my best to ignore it and shut it up, my body was still screaming that this wasn't right. My body knew that my dad's behavior wasn't normal; that what he was doing wasn't okay; that all the bullshit he had been feeding me for years was not true, at least not for me. In those moments when I allowed myself to pay attention to my body, the grossness of his behavior was clear: every time my dad came in, my body instantly tensed up, wanting to rebel and flee, to do anything to get away. I had to force myself to stand there under the water, tightly clenched, strangling that fight-or-flight instinct, pretending that everything was okay.

"Dad, can I just shower in private?" I tried nicely. "Dad, do you mind going back behind the curtain?" I asked with a smile. "Dad, would you please leave?" I finally said, showing the tiniest hint of frustration allowed, hoping maybe he would get the hint.

If he acknowledged my requests at all, it was always with a baffled, "No," delivered as if I was being stupid, like I was the one with the problem. "It's okay that I'm here, Becca. It's alright. It's normal. Why does it bother you? It shouldn't bother you." His responses made me feel small and confused, like I couldn't possibly understand what was appropriate for a father and his daughter, an adult and a child. Being in there with him was scary, but questioning him was scary too. And I didn't know what to do about the clear, certain opinions from my body, so I just kept trying to shut them down. At least, in my mind, I could somehow justify and excuse what was happening despite how uncomfortable it made me feel. What other options did I have? This was my dad, my home, where else could I go? Where else would I be safe? I didn't know what to do, but having his eyes on me felt like torture. With each visit, it felt more and more like I was dying a slow death on the inside, while, on the outside, the shell of my body, traitorously, kept developing into a woman.

2001

One evening when I was sixteen, my dad was there again, waiting and watching me shower. He was asking me questions, making me engage with him. There was a knock on the door, and then my mom poked her head in. She saw my dad.

Though I couldn't see her face, her voice clearly revealed her surprise and disgust. "You shouldn't be in here, Ron. You're bothering her. She's trying to shower."

"It's fine, we're just talking," he replied, brushing her off.

I noted the pregnant pause and then heard the door close as she slipped back into the hall, leaving us alone. That could have been my chance to finally tell her, to explain to her what I had been going through for years: how he had been invading my privacy and the way I felt trapped by him. A few minutes later, my dad left the bathroom. Thankfully, I was able to finish up and wrap myself in my towel without worrying about him. As I exited the shower, I could see my mom and dad talking in the kitchen, him quietly scolding her with terse words that *it was none of her business* and *how dare she interfere with how and where he talked to his children?* As I emerged from the bathroom into the hall, my mom looked over at me. I met her eyes and, with a quick glance at my dad, shyly said, "It's okay, Mom. It's not a big deal." Her expression said she didn't quite believe me, so I added, "Really. Don't worry about it."

Was I lying? I wasn't sure. On one hand, my dad said it was okay, and I wanted to believe that I could trust him—trust my dad. On the other hand, I couldn't deny how uncomfortable and awful it felt every time he entered the bathroom when I was in there. I told my mom it was okay because I didn't want to get in trouble with my dad, or to get her in trouble either. I was scared of what might happen if I suddenly confessed my true feelings about what he'd been doing and revealed the extent of his visits. So we all stood there in silence, the tension palpable. My mom gave me another look and then accepted my words and went to check on dinner. I don't know if she was scared, too, or if she just forgot, but my mom never mentioned it again, so neither did I.

After that night I noticed that my mom became extra quiet and withdrawn. I was worried about her, but I was also busy and distracted with school and sports and my own issues, so I didn't talk to her much about anything serious or substantial. She seemed exhausted, and I didn't want to burden her with my problems when she seemed miserable enough already. I realized that, if I wasn't able to tell my mom about the ongoing bathroom visits from my dad, then who *was* I supposed to tell? Who do you go to when something like that is happening? And what if the person I went to told me that this was all normal? That I *was* being ridiculous? Would they then tell my dad I had said something? What would the consequences of *that* be? Everyone at our church thought my dad was a good, upstanding Christian man, and they had seen us hugging and laughing together at youth group activities. Who would believe me when I said that he was watching me in the shower? Who would take *my* side if I said I didn't think it was okay? Who would believe these stories when it was the teenage daughter against her devout, righteous father? Who would believe me?

With my dad, I was always in the wrong, always incorrect—seeing, thinking, or feeling things that he said were not true or were inaccurate, or that I had no reason or right to think or feel. Even if I disagreed with him, I had to concede and apologize and accept what *he* said or believed to be true. My beliefs were irrelevant. And if my own father wouldn't trust me, if *I* could barely trust myself to know what was right, then why would I think anyone else would accept what I told them?

I knew, in my gut, that it was easier and safer to keep my feelings and thoughts to myself, to be agreeable and go along with what my dad told me. My body seemed to know the truth, but could I trust it? My dad expected me to be the dutiful, obedient daughter, and I knew that's what I was supposed to be, even if my body thought otherwise.

I wanted to do the right thing, but I wasn't sure I could trust myself to know what the right thing was. What if there's a conflict between what's right for me and what's right for someone else? How was I supposed to decide what was right when there were so many mixed messages? Was what my dad said always the right thing because he was a grown-up? What about when what seemed right for me would disappoint him or make him mad?

What about when someone else's "truth" feels like a lie?

STAND BY MY MAN

FEBRUARY 2009

After Stephanie's phone call revealed the extent of craziness that Jason was going through, he finally admitted to me that it was worse than he had initially let on. He told me how Stephanie's daughter was coming up with more and more lies about him. Neither Jason nor I understood why she hated him so much. "Becca, you would not believe the things she's saying," he'd told me later that week when he got home from work. "She hasn't been showing up to her shifts, right? Well, get this: today she texted me saying she thinks she's pregnant with my child. I mean, she is batshit crazy! This is ridiculous."

"What?!" I exclaimed, shocked that she was taking this to the next level. "Oh my god! What is her problem? Why is she doing this? This is insane!"

"I know," he complained. "Can you believe this shit?"

"We need to, I don't know . . . write all of this down or something. We need to keep track of all this shit she's saying. We should be documenting all of this." I found a notebook and flipped to a blank page. Grabbing a pen, I started writing down everything Jason had told me about what was going on. As I wrote, I became even more angry and disgusted with what Stephanie and her daughter were saying about Jason. I couldn't believe we had to deal with this. It was so unfair. I filled several pages with our notes and then slipped it into the drawer in our kitchen where we kept office supplies. I didn't want to have to look at it every day, but at least it would be close by if we needed it again.

The next day, my mom and I were at the restaurant help-ing Jason paint the storefront. I had already told her what Jason had been accused of, and as we painted, I vented my frustrations. "You would not believe the things she is saying, Mom. I just don't understand why she is doing this to him! And now," I added, "apparently, she thinks she might be *pregnant*." I rolled my eyes. "I wish she would just stop it, and just leave us alone!" I didn't say it, but I thought, *This girl needs to get over her stupid little destructive crush. He's mine, not hers!* Her com-mitment to this ridiculous storyline made me sick.

I wasn't *really* worried that Jason was cheating on me with her. I mean, I was a *woman*. She was just some teenager, prac-tically a child. I wasn't threatened by her, at least not in that way. But she *was* threatening the life Jason and I had together; this life that I had built, this beautiful normalcy I had created after all that crap with my father. Now, this girl's presence, her side of the story, her accusations, had the potential to destroy our life and our happiness.

As I talked, my mom didn't say much, just asked a few clari-fying questions. I think she could see that I wasn't ready to have an actual conversation. I really, truly did believe Jason—100 percent. There was no way this girl could possibly be telling the truth, a truth that would obliterate my life. I refused to entertain that idea. In my world, that possibility didn't even exist.

––––––––

The next day, I had a meeting at school with some other teachers. Stephanie was leading the discussion. She and I obviously knew what was happening with our families, but no one else did. The meeting was painfully uncomfortable, the tension between us palpable. I couldn't look her in the eye. Everyone could tell something was wrong, but of course, they couldn't possibly imagine the extent of it.

Stephanie was incredibly professional. Had I not been present, no one would have guessed there was a problem. At that moment, *I* was the problem. I was so angry at her, so utterly disgusted by what she and her daughter were doing to me and Jason.

Whereas Stephanie had once been like a mentor, now she was my mortal enemy. I would fight to the death to prove that her daughter was lying, but I would still be professional about it. I could not risk anyone else finding out about this. God forbid the news spread to the rest of the campus where the gossip train would load it up and spread it to all the other passengers. I didn't want anyone else to know about this or to think poorly of me or Jason. Or worse, to feel like they had to pick a side: me or Stephanie. I didn't want to have to answer any questions or defend myself or deal with other people's opinions. I had to keep this quiet. I had to keep my cool. If I acted out, there would be consequences; I might even lose my job. And we certainly didn't need *that* added to this mess.

At first, I thought I could avoid Stephanie (except for these meetings, of course). I would just keep to myself, eat lunch in my classroom, and distance myself on the playground at recess until all of this blew over. But after the meeting ended, I went back to my classroom seething with anger. Just being in her presence fueled my rage to a boiling point. I had to stop her and, in turn, stop her daughter. This was my *life* they were messing with, and my husband! I would not allow them to keep perpetuating these lies.

I marched back over to Stephanie's classroom, hoping all of the other teachers had left. I took a deep breath and slowly opened her door. The bright, cheerful reading skills charts and beautiful, calm poetry posters decorating her walls were interspersed with children's drawings and friendly class reminders. I knew Stephanie's intent was for this to be a peaceful, welcoming space for her students, but I felt like a warrior entering the gladiator pit.

She was sitting alone at her horseshoe-shaped table at the far end of the room where she had led our meeting just a few moments before, and looked up from her planner as I walked toward her. With each step, I tried to magic my anger into courage so that I could say the things I needed to say. Stephanie put her pen down and sat back in her chair, hands lightly folded on the desk. Her casual ease and openness caught me off guard, like my opponent had surrendered her sword.

I looked away from her, refocused my thoughts, and began speaking. I heard my voice shaking as I said, "I understand that you believe what your daughter is saying, but I believe my husband, and I am going to stand by him." A rush of strength surged through me. It felt noble, brave, *grown up*, to declare that I trusted my husband. "I will *not* let you or your daughter ruin my marriage with your lies," I said evenly, looking directly at her. "I respect you, and you do what you feel like you need to do, but I also need you to respect me and what I need to do."

My words hung in the air between us. Then she nodded, and gently replied, "I understand. And I need to stand by my daughter and do what is right for her."

I turned my face away again, staring at the wall as I tried to fight back tears. I stood there for a few more moments, but both of us were quiet. There was nothing more to say. The battle I had come to fight was ending in a stalemate. As I turned to go, I met her gaze once more, unprepared for the kindness and compassion I saw there. I stumbled back to my own classroom, tears blurring my eyes, and slammed the door behind me. My legs crumpled and I collapsed to the floor, sobbing. *Why is this happening? Why is this girl trying to destroy my marriage? Why won't Stephanie stop this? Can't they see what they are doing to me?*

The school bell rang loudly, and I heard the chatter of students as they began filling the hallways. I stood up, grabbed some tissues off my desk, and blotted my eyes and nose as best as I could. I had to believe that everything was going to be okay. I had to believe that the truth was going to come to light and we could go back to the way things were before. There was no other option. I trusted Jason. He loved me. We would deal with this crazy situation and move on and be happy. We would get through this. I took a sip of my Coke and pasted a smile on my face just as the kids came through the door.

All I could think to do was pretend that everything was okay. No matter what, I could not allow my job to be affected by these scandalous accusations against Jason. I didn't know how I would explain to someone why I could no longer be in the same room with Stephanie or why I felt like screaming and crying in the middle of the day. I just had to keep my shit together and everything would be fine. I would fake every interaction, pull a mask over my face and my body like I'd done with my father, and do whatever I had to do to project a normal, happy teacher and wife, living her normal, happy, uncomplicated life.

I was good at keeping secrets and, in this case, I had no other option. I stood at the head of the classroom, looked over my students taking their seats, and mentally donned what felt like a fifty-pound suit of armor. The weight of this facade felt heavy and awkward and confining but, hiding behind it, I knew I was safe.

QUIET DEFIANCE

2001

A s I was getting ready for school early one morning, I heard footsteps coming down the hall. My body tensed as the noise stopped and the door slowly opened. My sister's face peered around the edge, and she stepped into the bathroom. I gasped, then glared at her. "God, Beth! Why didn't you knock?!"

"Sorry," she said apologetically, closing the door and then coming to stand beside me.

She reached for a brush and began styling her hair. "So, did Dad walk in on you last night too?" she whispered. "Why does he do that? Ugh. I hate it. It's so . . . weird."

"Yeah, he did," I said, swiping mascara across my eyelashes and stepping back to take a final look at my makeup.

"I mean, why does he just stand there and talk? Blah, blah, blah," my sister mimicked his voice and made a face. I gave a little laugh, but as our eyes met in the mirror, we both turned serious.

"Let's just . . . look out for each other, okay?" I said quietly, trying not to make it a big deal, but hoping she would agree. She gave a slight nod and sighed heavily, before tossing the brush on the counter and heading to the kitchen for breakfast.

My sister and I loved each other, but we didn't always connect. She was being homeschooled through an online curriculum, and I had just started my junior year at the high school, so we didn't interact much during the day. We occasionally attended church activities together, but, for the most part, we lived separate lives. I often wished that we could just pack up our things and disappear, driving far away so we could escape our dad for good. The biggest obstacle to that dream, at least as I believed then, was that I didn't have my driver's license or much money of my own.

Having turned sixteen, I'd approached my dad about getting my license, since all my friends had already gotten theirs. "Oh come on, Becca," he said, looking at me with a condescending smile. "You don't even have a car. What would you do with your license?" He patted my hand. "You have your driver's permit. That's all you need for now." Of course *he* would say that. He wasn't the only junior who had to ask their parents to take them to volleyball tournaments or drop them off at football games. I knew it was petty, but I resented him even more as I renewed my learner's permit for the second time.

Seeing no possible escape, my sister and I developed strategies for dealing with our dad. We both started knocking and announcing ourselves when the other was in the bathroom or shower. We learned to speak with our expressions, silently communicating Dad's current mood by raising our eyebrows, rolling our eyes, or shaking our head in the subtlest gesture.

When we could, we hung out in the bathroom together, having realized my dad was less likely to interrupt when there were two of us. Maybe, we thought, he wouldn't want anyone else witnessing his behavior.

Those days, I was trying to get to school early, catching rides with friends or walking, anything to keep up my good-student persona and avoid time with my dad. Because of what I was enduring at home, school was my refuge. It felt even more important to me to be a great athlete, be a stellar student, and ace all my tests and projects. These parts of my life, at least, felt like things that I could control. I didn't see it as me trying to be perfect; I just wanted to be *normal*. And, in order to have a normal life—one without all this shame and uncertainty— I needed to have control over as many aspects of it as possible. I would do whatever was necessary to stay out of trouble, keep my nose clean, fly under the radar, and appear like everything was okay.

At school, I tried hard to act like the typical teenage girl. I laughed with friends and kissed my boyfriend like I had no cares in the world. I didn't talk to anyone about my dad's bathroom and shower visits. At this point, I wouldn't have even known *how* to talk about them. It was all so embarrassing. The people I hung out with were *normal*. They seemed to have good—or at least reasonably functioning—relationships with their parents. I didn't want to be different from them. I wanted to fit in, to be *normal* like they were. As long as I didn't tell them what was happening at home or give anyone cause for concern, I wouldn't stand out or draw unnecessary attention to myself. I could hide in the crowd, and no one would ever know. Turns out that when you're trying to be good, you can become—almost—blessedly invisible.

Or so I hoped.

———

It was stiflingly hot when I arrived home one afternoon that fall, sweaty and exhausted from a long day at school and a tough volleyball practice. My mom was out running errands and my dad wasn't home from work yet, so the house was empty. With sweat still dripping down my face and back, I quickly grabbed a change of clothes and headed for the bathroom.

Setting the clothes on the counter, I leaned down and turned the water on so it could warm up. I removed my sports bra and shorts as the sound of the water rushing out the tap became thunderous in the small room. Tension crept up my naked body, and my heartbeat slowed to a standstill. The air tightened around me, and I suddenly realized I was alone.

Alone.

Everything went quiet as I stepped over my discarded clothes, pulled the bathroom door shut, and turned the lock.

With that soft click, I released a deep breath, and my body relaxed completely. The air softened and I noticed the steam rising and fogging up the mirror. I lifted the shower pin and stepped into the tub, closing my eyes as the heat and sound of the water engulfed me.

I stood like that for several minutes, enjoying the feel of the water sliding over my skin, rinsing off the salty sweat, washing away the tension and stress of the day. Finally, I lifted my arms and reached for the shampoo.

Then the doorknob jiggled.

I stopped breathing, totally frozen in place. Seconds ticked by. The doorknob jiggled again. I dropped my arms to my sides and let my head droop, shoulders sagging, knowing my peaceful moment was over.

The whole room shook when my dad pounded his fist on the door. "Open the door!" he shouted. I couldn't move, couldn't speak. He beat the door with both fists, booms echoing, walls rattling, explosions happening all around me. "OPEN! THIS! DOOR!"

My heart raced. The water hurried down and over my body, as if it, too, wanted to run away. Fear gripped my throat as I remembered, *I was alone. It was just me.* Knowing I was defeated, I reached over and popped the lock.

My dad plowed through the door and threw back the shower curtain. "How dare you lock this door! This is MY house! You do NOT lock me out!"

I cowered in a ball under the flow of water. His face was reddish purple, eyes clouded with rage. As he continued to scream at me, his words blurred with the roar in my ears. But I got the message: I was not to test him again. *His* rule was law. What I thought or felt or needed or wanted didn't matter. No one locked him out of his own bathroom, especially not his daughter, not in his house! Finally, his fury spent, he turned and stormed out, pushing the door wide open as he left.

My heart pounded and my ears rang as I lay there in the tub that had begun to feel more and more like a cage. I don't know if I was there for a minute or an hour; if the water was still warm or had grown cold. I felt as though I was in another dimension, some altered reality where there was no air, no time, no meaning. Slowly, I moved from my crumpled position and pushed up to my hands and knees. My body wouldn't stop shaking, but at least I was breathing again.

Now that I had seen this side of my dad—a side I'd tried to pretend didn't exist—I could feel my body cracking open against my will, its truths starting to emerge from under the layers of shame that had been subtly and carefully constructed.

I wasn't sad, although anyone who saw me would have thought otherwise—I looked like a depressed and naked drowned rat hanging onto the edge of the tub. But no, I wasn't sad—and I wasn't angry. Inside of me, I felt a new strength building. Since the bathroom visits had started, I had been at war with myself, knowing that I had to accept how my dad treated me no matter how ashamed or scared it made me feel. For years, he had tried to convince me that I should feel the same way he did, that all of this was okay. But this time, my dad's behavior had summoned what felt like an ancient and awful truth within me, one that would no longer remain silent: I was not safe with him.

It felt like he wanted to defeat me, wanted to make me feel small. Yet, as I pushed myself up to stand under the still-flowing water, I felt like a warrior rising up to fight.

I couldn't talk for the rest of the night. I was afraid of what I might say, afraid of what would come out now that my fear had been replaced with this quiet defiance. I was uncertain about this new feeling, and didn't know how much I could trust it. Already, I could sense a shift in the battle within myself. This defiant feeling had arisen out of nowhere, entirely on its own, totally beyond my control, which automatically made it feel dangerous. Deep within, I knew that it was real, like some forgotten part of me was now making itself known.

As usual, I didn't mention the shower incident or this new, growing feeling inside of me to anyone. My silence was a way to keep it all under control. Besides, I told myself, other people had dealt with so much worse. Sure, my dad was a jerk and had anger issues and this stupid thing with the bathroom and shower, but it wasn't really abuse, was it? I wasn't being raped or molested. What if no one else thought it was as bad as I did? What if I was making this into a big deal and everyone else just brushed it off? I mean, all teenagers have issues with their parents, right? But even as I tried to convince myself that my situation wasn't that bad, the words rang hollow in my mind. And in the spaces in between, I could feel that quiet defiance breathing deep within me, reminding me that it was there and it was getting stronger.

DEVASTATED AND CONFUSED

2001

That Thursday afternoon was warm and sunny. My boy-friend had just pulled into our driveway to drop me off after school, when my sister came running out to meet me. I had barely stepped out of the car when she started talking. Her voice was quiet and concerned as she explained that she had tried to wake Mom up all day but had not been able to. "I think Mom's really sick," she said. "She moves around a little and mumbles things I can't understand, but she hasn't gotten out of bed."

"Did you call Dad?" I asked, distracted as I collected my backpack and said goodbye to my boyfriend.

"Well, I let her sleep in until around lunch but when she was still the same, I called Dad, like, five times. He didn't answer his office phone."

When we got into the house, I immediately dropped my bags and followed my sister to my parents' room. We found Mom exactly where she had been all day, flat on her back on her side of the bed, breathing shallowly. "Mom? It's me, Becca. It's time to get up," I said loudly, gently shaking her. Just as my sister had said, my mom stirred and muttered something, but didn't wake. Concern started to creep up my spine. What should we do? My dad had taken our little brother to school that morning and should have already picked him up by now. That meant they would be home any minute. I knew my mom slept a lot, but I had never seen her like this. I tried to rouse her again, to no response. Now, I didn't just feel worried, I felt scared. I thought about calling 911, but what good would that do? Would they want to send an ambulance? She didn't seem okay to me, but it also didn't seem like a medical emergency . . . Maybe we should just wait until my dad arrived.

Moments later, relief washed through me as I heard the front door open and my little brother's voice calling out as he and my dad came inside. I ran down the hall and accosted my dad in the same way my sister had me. "Dad! Mom's not getting up! Beth tried all day and she's not waking up!" My father barely glanced at us as he continued into the house and nudged my brother off to his room to play. "Dad!" I cried, "Did you hear me? Aren't you going to do anything?"

He set his jacket down on the couch and sighed with annoyance. "You know how she naps all the time. I'm sure nothing is wrong." He went into the kitchen, opened the refrigerator, and took out a drink, totally unconcerned.

Beth and I stood at the counter, facing him. "No! You don't

get it!" I said, my words coming out firmer and more confident than I felt. "Something is wrong! You need to take her to the hospital."

Beside me, Beth added, "Yeah, Dad, she's acting really strange. She's been asleep, like, all day."

Rolling his eyes, he said, "Look, you two. I'm not taking her to the hospital. There is nothing wrong."

"Fine! Then I'll take her!" I declared.

He scoffed, "You don't have your license yet. You can't drive anywhere."

"Watch me!" I glared into his eyes, hoping that my stubbornness wouldn't get me into trouble, but would trigger him to take action and actually listen to us.

He set his drink down and studied my face. "Girls, I'm sure your mother is fine. You don't need to overreact like this and take her anywhere." He waved his hand dismissively. "Look, if for some reason she is still like this in the morning—which she won't be—but if she is, I'll take her to a doctor myself. Okay?"

My sister and I looked at each other. I felt so conflicted. I was used to my dad belittling my feelings and making me second-guess myself, but this was different. This was my mom. She looked so weird there in bed, unmoving and distant.

"What do we do?" Beth whispered to me when my dad had left the room. I shook my head. I didn't know. I had tried to stand up to him and was shut down. I didn't know if I wanted to risk stealing the car keys and, even so, how would we get my mom to the car if she couldn't walk? I felt stuck, and my sister's face told me she felt the same.

As the evening dragged on, Beth and I took turns going in and checking on Mom. Asking Dad for an update seemed pointless, and I wanted to see her with my own eyes. It was way past my bedtime and there was still no change, so I went to bed hoping that Mom would be back to normal in the morning. That she would be up and smiling before I headed off to school; that maybe she had just had a really bad virus and it had passed.

I woke up the next day, instantly sensing that something was wrong. It felt too quiet in the house, and as I strained my ears I could hear strange voices coming from the other room. With my body on high alert, I jumped out of bed and strode down the hall to the kitchen.

My dad was at the sink, washing dishes. Standing near him were two people from our church. Although they smiled kindly at me, I felt suspicious of them and confused. I turned back to my dad. "Good morning," he said, then added, "As soon as your sister gets up, I need to talk to you both."

I looked around, realizing who wasn't there. "Where's Mom? Did you take her to the hospital?" I asked.

His voice sounded distant and stiff as he answered, "Yes. That's what I want to talk to you about."

I ate my cereal in silence while the adults talked quietly and milled around. *Is he telling me the truth?* If he had taken her to the hospital, it must be serious. I didn't want to breathe until I knew she was okay. She was my safety net. A source of comfort and consistency, someone who loved me no matter what. She and my sister were like my fellow prisoners, all forced to share this insufferable space around my dad. I hadn't seen her eyes in two days, and her absence felt like a gaping hole inside of me.

"Becca!" My dad's voice snapped me back into alertness. When I looked up, I saw that Beth had woken, and he tipped his head toward the hall, saying, "Why don't we all go into the living room and sit on the couch?"

I followed him and took a seat next to my sister, while he sat in a chair across from us. The people from church stood in the doorway, forming a little circle that I think was supposed to be comforting, but instead felt like a trap.

My dad huffed out a breath, then began to speak. "Girls, your mom took too much of her medicine. That's why she didn't respond when we tried to wake her up. She was still unconscious early this morning, so I took her to the hospital. They pumped her stomach and she's going to be okay—but she's going to need to stay at the hospital for a while, so the doctors can monitor her." His voice caught and one of the church people stepped over to gently touch his shoulder, comforting him.

Tears spilled down my cheeks as I took in his words. I gripped my sister's hand. We had known something was wrong. My anger at him for not listening to us mixed with sadness and concern for my mom. I felt as if everything in me was stretched taut, like a rubber band ready to snap. "Can we go see her?" I whispered hopefully, trying to be strong. It was the only thing I wanted at that moment: to see my mom. To touch her, smell her, know that she was real and alive and okay. My dad was being way too calm, way too nice. He hadn't even wanted to take her yesterday and now he was acting so sad. Something else was going on here, but I didn't know exactly what it was. The people from church were there, which would definitely put him on his best behavior, but that didn't seem to explain all of it.

"Sweetie," he replied, deepening the suspicion that was rising inside of me—he was *never* this nice to us—"I'm going to go back to the hospital to check on her. These guys will stay here with you. There will be some other people bringing some meals over later today and then I'll be home tonight. Your grandma is on her way too. Everything's gonna be fine." With that, he stood up and was immediately pulled into his friend's embrace, before getting his keys to leave for the hospital.

I felt swallowed up by despair and grief, and also a flash of anger that he wouldn't take me to see her.

The day dragged on just like the night before. It was the longest, slowest day of my life. People came and went: a food brigade piling casseroles and snack plates on our kitchen counter; others rearranging our fridge and pantry to make space. I sat in the living room trying to listen to the truth that was hidden beneath this. I knew we were not getting the whole story. My ears strained for hints, but I could only hear low muttering around me, like everyone was afraid to speak too loudly. My nerves seemed to crawl out of my skin, trying to feel into this atmosphere of secrecy, but everything just blurred together. All I could do was wait.

The next day, we were allowed to go see her. We got dressed, loaded into the car, and headed to the hospital. Everyone was moving too slowly for me. I felt like I couldn't get to her fast enough. As we entered the cold, stark lobby, I couldn't stop twisting my hands and looking around, unable to be still, everything in me wanting to be where she was *now*.

We arrived at a secured door and a nurse buzzed us in. My eyes searched along the hallway, wondering which room my mom was in. I heard my dad talking to the nurse and then heard my name.

"What?" I asked, turning around. My attention fell on the nurse who stood behind the desk, examining our little group.

A moment later, she gently asked, "Do any of you have any glass or anything sharp with you?" I exchanged glances with my dad and sister, and we all shook our heads no. "What about any toys, or pens, or anything with small pieces that could be broken off?" Again, no.

Then she looked down at my shoes and told me I had to take them off.

"Why?" I asked, totally baffled at the request.

"I need you to please take the shoelaces out of your shoes and give them to me. Then you can wear your shoes in."

What? Why the fuck do you need my shoelaces? I thought angrily. I didn't actually say that, of course, but I'm pretty sure my face gave me away. I looked to my dad so he could explain to the nurse how ridiculous and unnecessary this was, but instead, he bent his head toward mine and quietly revealed the secret.

"Your mom is on suicide watch. We can't bring anything into her room that she could possibly use to harm herself."

There it was: the truth.

My mom hadn't "accidentally" taken too much medicine; she had *purposely* taken too much medicine. She had tried to kill herself. I knew she loved me, loved all of us. But how could these two facts coexist? She loves us, but she tried to kill herself. *Why would she do that?*

Stunned into silence, I reached down and unlaced my shoes, willing myself not to cry. As I stood up, I took a deep breath and handed them to the nurse, bracing myself. My mom was still here. She was still alive. I could do this.

The nurse took the shoelaces and then led us to my mom.

From the doorway, I could see her lying there in the bed. She looked dead. Her face was pale, her lips blue. She had oxygen tubes in her nose, snaking back and around her ears, and multiple IVs in her hands and arms, secured with tape. Her eyes were closed and the wrinkled, wave-like, paper-thin texture of her eyelids made it seem like she might blow away. Her hair was greasy and stuck to her forehead. I stepped up to her side and brushed her hair back, hoping she knew it was me.

She opened her eyes and turned to look at me. In that moment, I saw life come back into her, just a little, as she gave me a tiny smile. Tears trickled from the corners of her eyes, and I slid my hand into hers. She squeezed my fingers, but her grip faded and her eyes dulled as soon as my dad entered the room. She turned her face to me again, but it wasn't the same. The light had gone out.

I thought she was tired, or maybe in pain, so I laid her hand gently on the sheet and stepped to the side. At least she was here. I still had my mom. I had seen her face, touched her hand, and got full confirmation that she was alive. And something in me knew that she wasn't going to leave me in this world without her. She would come home.

———

My mom was in the hospital for two weeks. I was a robot, going through the motions, still trying to pretend that my life was normal. I went to school, hung out with friends, went to my lifeguarding job at our local pool, came home, ate dinner, stared at the ceiling, wondered why she would want to leave us and continuously tried to understand her actions. My dad and Grams said that when Mom came home, we needed to help around the house and make things easier for her. We were to be more quiet, more helpful, not fight with each other, and not be too demanding. Basically, we should try not to exist.

When the car pulled into the driveway with my mom inside, I ran to the door, so glad and relieved she was with us again. I watched her get out of the car, helped by my Grams, and realized that, while she was obviously my mom, something about her was different. She looked . . . weary, heavy. Her face lit up when she saw us, but that fading thing happened again as she moved past me and into the house.

Friends from church stopped by to see her. "How are you doing?" they asked, concern in their voices. They were waiting to help. They wanted to *fix* her.

46

"I'm fine, I'm fine. Getting better every day," she would say, smiling brightly. Later, I would see her curled up on the couch, looking small and fragile, her expression blank.

My dad was playing his role like an award-winning actor. He was the distraught husband of a wife who had tried to kill herself. Poor him, he would have been left all alone. He was sad and going through so much, what with having to take care of the children and the house too. His marriage was struggling because of what she had done; how would they recover? Everyone at church always said that suicide was a sin, a selfish act by someone who didn't understand God's goodness in their life. I could see the questioning in their faces: how could my mom have had such little faith? How could she have been so depressed, so misunderstanding of God's will that she would try to take her own life?

My dad's audience bought it all, believing his version of the story was true. Meanwhile, my mom sat there silently, letting his voice fill the room.

A few months after she was released from the hospital, my mom took a part-time job at a nearby bakery, her first job outside of the home in years. To most people, it looked like she was taking care of herself, taking an interest in life. I was glad she was seeking out new experiences and doing something that she enjoyed. She made new friends, became really good at baking, and started spending more time away from home. She seemed so much happier, but I watched my mom like a hawk, instantly attuned to the slightest change in her mood.

With my mom seemingly returning to her old self, my dad also appeared to have mellowed. I didn't fully trust the change, but despite everything he'd done, it was kind of nice to feel like I could talk to and be okay around him again, like a normal daughter with her father. He even surprised me one day by tossing me the keys to his Nissan Pathfinder.

"What are these for?" I asked, confused.

"Keep 'em. They're yours now."

My eyebrows shot up, as I stared at him, mouth agape. *What?*

"I decided I want something different. You can have the Pathfinder. Now that you've got a car, you can get your license."

To say I was shocked is an understatement, but I wasn't going to argue. I eagerly claimed the car and registered to take my driving test as soon as possible.

Things were so calm and quiet around our house that I actually had time to think more seriously about college. One morning, over breakfast, I was sitting at our dining room table, eating and staring out the large sliding glass doors to the backyard, thinking about what field of study I might want to go into. I was really enjoying the interior design class that I was taking at school, learning color theory and design elements, designing floor plans, and creating mood boards. It was as if time stood still whenever I was fully engrossed in that creative bubble. Interior design seemed like it could be an exciting career to go into. As I daydreamed, a sense of possibility rose inside of me.

My dad came in and sat down at the other end of the table from me. "Good morning," he said.

"Morning," I replied, trying to determine if now was a good time to talk to him about my college plans. His face was even, and he seemed to be calm as he ate his cereal, so it seemed as good a time as any.

"So, I was thinking," I began. "I've been loving my interior design class and I think I really have a talent for it. The teacher thinks so too." He nodded, like he was really listening, so I kept talking. "Since I'll be starting to fill out college applications soon, I've been thinking a lot about what program I want to apply for. I think interior design could be a really good option, and—"

My dad held up his hand, silencing me. "Well now, hold on just a minute," he interrupted. He wasn't angry, but he gave me a parental smile like I should know better. "Interior design isn't really a career or something to study in college. It's more of a hobby. Interior designers are not in high demand, and a career doing that would not put bread on the table." He explained that I should be very concerned about money, about providing for my family, about having a secure, stable, and reputable career. "There are other lucrative jobs out there, Becca," he assured me. "Doing something like interior design—well, let's just say that would be pretty irresponsible."

Ouch. His words stung. I didn't want to be irresponsible or have a job that didn't pay well and wouldn't allow me to take care of my future family. As he spoke, I felt kind of stupid. *Maybe I haven't thought this through well enough. Maybe I haven't actually considered all the elements.* My dad had a good paying job, after all, which provided for our family and allowed my mom to stay at home to take care of us. Wasn't that what I wanted too? Maybe he was right. Maybe interior design wasn't the best idea.

"Engineering is a much better field to get into," he continued. "Engineers are well paid, in high demand, and the jobs are very stable. It's a fool-proof route; a very responsible choice, I think. Give it some thought. You really don't want to set yourself up for failure." He finished his cereal, took his bowl to the sink, and got ready to head off to work. The picture-perfect image of the man of the house doing what he needed to do for his family.

I mulled over our conversation. I did love interior design, but maybe it didn't have to be a career. Maybe it could just be my hobby, like he'd said. I could apply what I was learning in my own house, someday, or perhaps help my friends. Being an engineer could be fun, I guess . . . I mean, I was good at math. And like he'd said, in the end, it seemed like it would be better and more responsible, to have the certainty and security that came with an engineering degree. I left for school feeling disappointed, but knowing my dad was probably right.

———

Each week, my mom had a counseling appointment and spent time connecting with others in an online support group chat room. I continued to see a new strength building in her. I had noticed that she wasn't as easily controlled by my dad anymore. For as long as I could remember, when he asked her to do something, she did it immediately, jumping up and dropping everything to do whatever it was he wanted. She seemed to be afraid of what might happen if she didn't respond right away. The consequences of disobeying or challenging him could be subtle and quiet, or obvious and loud. He might belittle her under his breath or through clenched teeth, or shout through the house and set everyone on edge.

Despite his past unpredictable behavior, now my mom was setting time limits. When he told her she needed to change over the laundry, she'd reply firmly, "I can do that in ten minutes, when I'm finished with my book." When he insisted that he needed to talk to her *right now*, she'd look him in the eye and say, "I'll talk for fifteen minutes, Ron, but then I have some other things to do."

He never responded, at least not like he would have before. Instead, I could see the veins in his neck grow taut and his eyes twitch and narrow. I could tell he wanted to react, but he also really seemed to be making an effort to play his new role of the sad, loving husband. The victim.

I carefully watched how these new interactions between them played out. You didn't say no to my dad. *He* didn't wait. I could feel the energy in the room shift whenever my mom set these boundaries. When he didn't fight her or publicly confront her about them, I began to wonder if we could start setting boundaries with him too.

But I didn't get a chance to test it. Unfortunately, as time went on, the more my mom stood up for herself and the more independent she became, the more my dad started to take his anger out on me and my sister. That calm, caring facade he'd been wearing for the last six months suddenly vanished.

"Do *not* walk away when I'm talking to you!" he yelled when we innocently thought a conversation was over. "Do *not* leave your clothes on the floor!" "Get back in here!" "You are *not* excused from the table!" Over and over and over. We left for school too early; we came home too late. We played our music too loud. We left our rooms too messy. There was no pleasing him, and no asserting control when he made it clear that *he* was the one in charge.

My mom and I were in the kitchen once when my dad came up behind her. Although he had resumed his nastiness with Beth and me, he still mostly treated my mom with kid gloves. He wrapped his arms around her waist and kissed her neck. My mom froze, like he had just zipped her up in a straitjacket. He spoke to her like she was a small child, making his voice higher than normal. She grimaced and cautiously slipped out of his embrace just as he raised his hands to begin rubbing her shoulders.

I stood there, awkward and uncomfortable, feeling like it was a private moment between them, but also recognizing that my mom did not want him touching her. I didn't know what to do. I looked at my mom, who now had her eyes closed while he massaged her neck. The micro-expression on her face was not one of relaxation, but of pain.

I turned away and opened the pantry to grab a snack. Stuck to the inside of the cabinet door was a "love" note from my dad to my mom. My stomach retched, my gut instantly telling me it was fake. *All of it* was so fake. I should have realized it months ago. He had *never* behaved this way with her before or been so nice to any of us. Sure, it was entirely possible for someone to suddenly change their behavior, but the way he was behaving now made him seem even more like Jekyll and Hyde. Who was he, really? Was he the loving husband and father who rubbed his wife's shoulders and called his daughters "sweetie" and gave them a car? Or was he the creep who watched me pee, the angry tyrant who shouted at me in the shower, and the condescending jerk who had belittled my mom for decades? I knew, instinctively, that whatever that act had been with us and that he was still continuing with my mom, it was not real.

Disgusted, I closed the cabinet and faced my parents again. My dad was still behind my mom, his hand on the small of her back as she stood at the counter. When I met her eyes, I knew. She didn't want him. She didn't want any of it. I immediately thought back to all the times my dad had ridiculed her, dismissed her, criticized her. He had beaten her down mentally and emotionally, just like he was doing to me. She, too, was trapped, and had been for so much longer, and so much more painfully. My breath caught and I had to leave the room as the realization hit me: She hadn't tried to commit suicide because she was depressed, like my dad had been saying. She had tried to escape him.

———

Over the next few weeks, I didn't know how to process this new insight into my mom. What was I supposed to do with a dad who held me hostage in the bathroom and a mom who had tried to kill herself? I was pretty sure none of my friends were dealing with anything like this. If I let myself think about it too much, I felt totally helpless and overwhelmed with sadness and fear. So, I did everything I could to distract myself.

I became really good at being busy. I mean *really* good—like expert-level busy. I got creative finding things to do: I asked my teachers for extra assignments and volunteered to do the most work on group projects. "Can I make two posters for this instead of just one?" I'd ask my teachers, who appeared to believe I was *extremely* engaged with the lesson and a self-motivated learner. I was industrious at work too—at the pool, I diligently checked the chlorine levels, studied up on first aid strategies, cleaned the bathrooms, and organized and reorganized the lost and found. I vigorously cleaned my room and worked out harder and longer. Being still was torture. Being told I had to read a book for school could invoke a near-panic attack: *you mean I have to just sit there—in silence!?* I breathed an audible sigh of relief when my teachers explained that we would read together in class. *Phew.* At least there would be other distractions, other people around. It wouldn't just be me alone with a book—and my thoughts.

Before too long, I noticed that the more efficient and organized and productive I was, the more people respected and rewarded me. I was just trying to distract myself from the internal shitshow I was experiencing, but the external validation felt pretty good too. I also understood that, if I was getting positive feedback for this behavior, then clearly, no one had any idea how fucked up I really was. My plan was working: as far as everyone else was concerned, I was on the "good" side of normal.

2002

One day, my mom came home with a new car, smaller and less expensive than her minivan. I learned later that she had opened up a bank account in her name only and had been depositing her paychecks there. Not long after that, my mom moved out. It happened so suddenly, I barely remember it. One minute she was there, the next thing I knew, she was gone, taking her things and my little brother with her.

"Your mom didn't want to live with us anymore, so she left," my dad told us. "She doesn't have the money or the room for you girls, so you're staying here with me."

Hmm. That didn't sound right, but I couldn't ask my mom about it now, since she wasn't there. All I had was my dad's side of the story. I didn't fully believe him, but I didn't know what to think. I still felt haunted by the sight of my mom in that hospital bed, the lifelessness in her body, so secretly, I was happy that she had finally escaped my dad's prison. Yet now, I felt abandoned and stuck here with him. I understood her actions, but at the same time, I was devastated by them. I wanted to ask her why she had moved out, why she hadn't taken us with her, but I didn't want to risk doing or saying anything that might make her feel bad or unloved or stressed out. Also, deep down, I was worried about what she *would* say. Maybe my dad was right. Maybe she didn't have room for us . . . maybe she didn't even want to *make room* for us.

Soon after my mom left, my dad announced that they were getting divorced. Ah, I thought, maybe she was just waiting for that to be finalized before she came back to get me and Beth. A few weeks later, my dad dashed all of my remaining hope. "I found out your mom has a new *roommate*," he spat, clearly disgusted by the idea. I stopped in my tracks, taken aback by this new information. I pictured her small place, so clear in my mind, even though we'd only visited a few times. I imagined the extra bedroom filled with someone else's stuff; the tiny kitchen cluttered with someone else's dirty dishes; the closet overflowing with someone else's clothes. All the empty spaces of my mom's life occupied by someone else. My breath caught as I tried not to cry. I felt painfully clear, now, that there definitely would not be any room in her apartment for me.

SNAPPED

2002

My mom's absence came as a shock to our household. She had taken care of so many things that we hadn't really been taught to do, like cooking and doing laundry. We may have had a few quick lessons, but she always felt it was more important for us to focus on our schoolwork. Without her there, I sometimes tried to make dinner, hesitantly offering dry pork chops smothered in barbecue sauce or overcooked noodles drenched in cream of mushroom soup to whoever happened to be home. Beth and I did our best to figure out the laundry situation too. Neither of us wanted to risk angering our dad because he didn't have clean underwear or because dinner wasn't on the table.

With my dad's moods becoming more and more unpredictable, I did everything I could to stay on his good side or avoid him altogether. I was eighteen and about to graduate.

I should have felt like I was on top of the world, but instead, I was like a ghost traveling through my life. A shadow of myself, barely visible. Don't show up too much, don't fade away completely. I was careful to not spend too much time in the bathroom lest I be subject to yet another one of my dad's visits. It felt like I tiptoed around the house all the time, and at school, I just tried to maintain the status quo so there was no reason for anyone to ask any questions. Laugh when a laugh is expected, meet school deadlines, don't ditch practice or miss work. Don't give anyone a reason to think anything is out of order.

My first strategy was always to avoid my dad whenever possible; my second was to anticipate what would set him off so I could minimize the likelihood of that happening. I wasn't sure what he would do if he got *really* mad at me. I knew that messy spaces were one of his biggest triggers, so I kept my room and the common areas mostly clean, knowing he would get upset if I didn't. My sister, on the other hand, often left her clothes all over the floor, and she and my dad constantly fought about it.

One afternoon, I heard them arguing in the dining room. I stealthily looked around the corner to see a laundry basket on the ground next to my sister's feet and my dad standing over her, yelling, his rage reverberating through the house. My sister bent down to get the basket and he pushed her onto the tiled floor. She spun around on her butt and faced him again. My throat tightened, hands clenched, eyes wide. *Oh my god, what is he going to do?*

He plucked a towel from the basket and wrapped it around his hand. His words now becoming incomprehensible, he started whipping the towel at my sister. Her arms and hands flew up to protect her face as he snapped the towel in rapid-fire shots, once, twice, ten times, so fast I hardly realized what was happening.

"Stop! Stop, Dad! Stop it!" I screamed, finally finding my voice, though I was shaking with fear. "Stop!"

He looked back at me, then threw down the towel and stormed off, leaving both my sister and I crying in his wake. I helped her up and led her back to her room. We sat on her bed in silence, holding hands. "You're gonna be okay," I whispered. "We'll figure this out." I brushed her hair back from her face, thankful not to see any red marks there. She seemed like she wanted to be alone, so I gave her a little hug and said, "I'll be in my room if you need me, okay?" She wiped her tears and nodded.

As I softly closed her door, I tried to process what I'd just seen. My dad had been an asshole in so many ways, but he'd never hit us. He'd never been physically violent. This was something new. We had to get out before it escalated. But how could we leave when we still needed him? We needed him to put a roof over our heads, to buy us food and clothes. And though I hated to admit it, I still wanted his love, needed him to love me. I didn't understand it—how could I hate him and resent him for everything he had done, and yet still keep hoping that he would somehow turn into a caring, compassionate, and supportive father? Would I ever have that?

When I got back to my room, I heard a car door shut. Looking outside, I saw my dad driving away, probably heading off to some church production, pasting on his fake smile, laughing and joking with the pastors, while we were left here, feeling trapped by his anger, abandoned by our mom, together and yet totally alone in the world.

———

"Hello?!? Earth to Becca!"

My head jerked up, as I looked toward the voice. I'd been so intent on reviewing my college applications that I didn't realize I had zoned out. "Sorry, what's up?" I asked, trying to refocus.

I was the manager-on-duty at our local swimming pool and, apparently, there was something I needed to deal with. "I'll be right there," I reassured the lifeguard, rubbing my eyes and trying to ignore the constant ache of dread in my stomach. As I left the office, I passed some other lifeguards walking out to their stations for the last shift of the night, their voices light and excited as they talked about our upcoming prom. My head pounded, but I tried to smile at them, to act normal. I watched the girls take their places and wished I could be like them. Nothing to worry about except homework, boys, and what I'd wear to the dance.

As I stepped outside to attend to the maintenance system— yet another challenging situation I was expected to know how to deal with—it suddenly all felt like too much. I couldn't do this anymore. How was I supposed to keep going when everything hurt? It was as if stones of grief and sadness were piling on top of me, breaking my bones; I was being crushed under the weight of my life.

I thought of my mom, and wondered if maybe this was how she had felt. Part of me hated that I was even having those thoughts, because all I had ever heard was that suicide meant you were weak and would go to hell . . . but I couldn't help it. Escaping all of this shit sounded really, really nice. Tears stung my eyes and I practically ran to the bathroom, locking myself in a stall and slumping onto the toilet. Sobs racked my body in waves, but I didn't want anyone to hear me. I didn't want anyone to ask what was wrong. There was no possible way to explain.

What the fuck was I supposed to tell them? What would they think if I did? And how could I even start the story when it had been going for years?! No one could possibly understand the hell I had been going through; how unloved and confused and angry I felt. No one could help me. What was the point?

I stood up quickly, anger now coursing through my veins. Screw this! Fuck it! No one cared if I was here or not, so why shouldn't I just end it? Just make it all stop? I was worthless. No one ever listened to me. No one wanted me. My life was just a big hot fucking mess.

I swung my work keys off of the lifeguard fanny pack around my waist and held the largest key in my right hand. It looked like a razor. I turned up my left wrist and touched the cold metal to my skin. My mind flashed to my mom, my sister, all of my desperate wishing that life could be different. I closed my eyes and swiped the key. It made a faint pink line on my wrist. It didn't even break the skin.

Are you fucking kidding me?!? Can't even just one thing work out for me?!?

I ground my teeth together and angrily sawed the key into my flesh. A trickle of blood appeared and I pushed harder. I gouged my skin, using as much force as I could muster.

Then, there was a shout. "Becca! Are you in here? Where are you?" Shit, my coworkers were looking for me.

I froze and held my breath. "Sorry! I'll be right out!" I called back, their interruption jolting me out of the moment. I looked down at the bruised, red skin on my arm, feeling both disappointed and relieved. I put my keys back in my pack, leaving the stall to splash water on my tear-stained face and wash my hands—I had to keep up the facade—then left the bathroom to start closing down the pool.

No one noticed what I had done. I couldn't decide if that made me feel better or worse. I put a Band-Aid over the reddest part of my wrist and tried to keep my arm hidden. I finished up my duties, made sure everyone was gone, and locked up the building.

I sat in my car for a while and thought about my life and what I had done. Well, what I had tried to do. I felt numb and hollow, staring blankly out my windshield. Since it was late and I hadn't eaten dinner, I went to Jack in the Box for tacos, and then I went home. My wrist was starting to hurt. In the pool bathroom, I had felt somber yet empowered, taking control and finding a way to make the pain and suffering stop. But now, I felt stupid and ashamed. My arm hurt really, really bad. In trying to take my pain away, I had just caused myself more.

As I lay in bed, running my fingers over my bandaged wrist, all these thoughts about being unworthy and unloved and unwanted and unsafe kept swirling around in my mind. Because of my mom, I knew that actual suicide was a real, possible option. But was it the only one? My mom had been able to figure things out. She had gotten a job and a new place to live, divorced my dad. From the little I had seen of her since then, it seemed like she was happier. And I was so thankful that she was still alive. My life really sucked right now, and I had no fucking clue what to do about any of it, but maybe I could figure it out too.

I was so tired. So fucking tired of my life, my dad and all his bullshit. I decided that I wanted to find a way out of this. There had to be a better option. I was strong, I was resilient, and I had survived shitty situations before. I could do it again.

———

"So, girls," my dad began, as he started up the car, pausing to smile and wave to the others who were also leaving the church parking lot. "We need to talk about the house." It had been a few weeks since the towel-whipping incident, and things had gotten worse at home. I turned and looked over at my sister in the back seat, rolling my eyes, no longer looking forward to this drive home. "I've been really disappointed with how you haven't been taking care of your things. It's not my job to pick up after you all the time."

He went on complaining, droning on and on about how lazy we were, how we didn't listen and didn't appreciate what he did for us, blah, blah, blah. I stared out the window, watching the blurry world go by. What he was saying in the car, at that moment, was benign enough. Normal dad stuff. But all I could see in my mind's eye was me hunched over the toilet as my dad pushed open the bathroom door; his eyes roving my body as he watched me in the shower; him whipping my sister; banging on the door; my mom in the hospital, her eyes dull and gray. Looking down at my healing wrist, I remembered how tired I was of this and how I wanted my life to be different.

A primal energy began thrumming inside of me. That quiet defiance I had managed to suppress was now writhing in my body, waking up, expanding by the second. I could feel the pressure of it like a physical force, my body suddenly seeming too small to contain it. My heart beat faster and I knew what I had to do. I had to get away from this man.

The next time we pulled up to a stop sign, I quickly opened the car door and got out. I slammed the door shut behind me and stepped onto the sidewalk, briefly taking in the neighborhood where we were, just blocks away from home. I did not run. I faced the car and saw that my dad had set the brake and was storming around the back end to approach me.

For a moment, everything seemed to move in slow motion. My dad's red, furious face and tense body were a wild contrast to the green lawns and idyllic, picture-perfect houses that surrounded us. I didn't have a plan for what I would do—I hadn't thought that far ahead—but, strangely, I felt safe.

Then, he was grabbing my arm and pulling me toward the car. "Get back in the car right now! I'm tired of this shit!" I dug in my heels as he yanked. "Get back in the fucking car!"

I struggled to free my arm from his grasp. "Don't touch me!" I snarled. Somehow, I knew that I needed to match his intensity. He let go of my arm but stepped closer, towering over me, flailing his arms and yelling in my face. I couldn't understand what he was saying, couldn't hear him clearly. It was the same as when he had yelled at me in the shower—no, not the same. *He* was the same. *I* was not.

I looked him in the eye, knowing that my rebellion was dangerous, but I was *done*. Head and chin tilted up defiantly, I stood there, silent and unmoving, as he rained down his barrage of insults and demands. "This is your last chance!" he shouted. "Get your ass back in the fucking car!"

"No," I proclaimed from clenched teeth, nostrils flaring.

Just past him, I could see Beth, who was now out of the car as well, watching us. We locked eyes and I knew we were in this together. My dad huffed one final time and spun around. He pushed past my sister, got back in the car, and waited.

For minutes, my sister and I just looked at each other, neither of us able to trust our legs to walk. I knelt down on the sidewalk, and she came up and wrapped her arms around me. Entangled like that, we cried. But they weren't sad tears. I had stood up to him. I had said no.

"I love you, Becca," Beth said, gently. "I am so proud of you."

"I know," I whispered. "I'm proud of you, too, and I love you so much." I turned to face her. "We have to get out of that house. We have to get out."

She nodded and I could see the determination I felt reflected in her eyes. "We will."

We stood and remained glued together for support. As we started to walk home, my dad trailed behind in the car. He pulled up alongside us and rolled down the window. "Girls, get back in the car, you don't need to do this. I was just joking. Get back in." Ignoring him, we kept walking. "Hey! I'm talking to you! Get back in the car! Stop being so sensitive!" he shouted. When we didn't respond, he swerved away from the curb and sped off.

We stayed mostly silent, quietly brainstorming our own plans to leave now that we knew *what* we needed to do. The *how* would come—it had to. We arrived home to find the house empty. We disappeared into our rooms, needing the space to decompress and think. When our dad returned later that evening, we all avoided each other and didn't talk, ignoring the ridiculously large elephant in the room. My dad never acknowledged the incident, which was fine with me, because I would never ever forget it.

SOMETHING NEW

2002

don't think I realized just how much I missed my mom. We hadn't seen her very much after she moved out, but eventually, once she got settled, she started inviting us over to her apartment. Slowly, I began spending more and more time over there. I stopped by after school or hung out with her on the weekends. Then she got a job working the snack register at my school cafeteria as my senior year of high school began. That meant I saw her at lunchtime, and sometimes I even stood next to her while she worked so we could chat. We weren't able to talk about anything deep and meaningful (not that we had ever done much of that, anyway) but seeing her every day and being able to talk to her about my classes and friends felt like such a relief.

Our meetings were clumsy and uncomfortable at first, because there were so many things that were still going unsaid.

But with every short conversation, the tension between us dissolved and that familiar sense of comfort and ease returned. These daily interactions at school brought a consistency and convenience to our relationship that I had really missed. I remembered the days when I would come home and lay on the cool kitchen tile after volleyball or track practice, and talk to her while she made dinner. Now, we weren't having any real heart-to-heart conversations, but seeing her and being with her at lunch became a touch-point for me and a reason for me to keep enduring despite what was still going on at home.

Seeing my mom's happiness and freedom renewed my own motivation to move out. Part of my plan was to make as much money as possible, as quickly as I could, even if it meant giving up sports. To my coaches' surprise, I stopped playing volleyball and running track in favor of a work-study program. When I explained that I needed to save for college, they just nodded in understanding and, thankfully, didn't ask any more questions. One of the times when I had stood up to my dad, he'd gotten so angry with me that he said he wouldn't pay for school. I could continue living at the house, but any college expenses would be my responsibility. I didn't know if he was totally serious, but I didn't want to risk finding out. For the rest of the year, I spent my afternoons either lifeguarding and managing the public pool or working at the credit union as a bank teller. I wasn't exactly sure what I was saving for or working toward, though. With my mom's suicide attempt, the divorce, and the resulting turmoil that happened my junior year, I had not submitted my college applications and had missed the key deadlines.

I lay awake at night wondering what to do. I was desperate to get away from my dad, but I also fully believed that getting a degree was my best chance at long-term success. I decided to attend our local community college, so I could do my prerequisites and work full time, with the intent of transferring somewhere else as soon as I could afford it. I was determined to shove it in my father's face that I could do college—and life—without his help. I would be financially responsible for all of my tuition and get out of his house as fast as I could. With this plan in place, I eagerly enrolled as a full-time college student and increased my work hours. I spent as little time as possible at home, and as much time as possible preparing for my escape.

2003

Living in my dad's house during college wasn't as bad as it had been in the past. Since I was so busy, I simply scheduled my life so that I came home after he was asleep and left before he woke up. I hardly ever saw him and he hardly ever saw me.

As the second semester began and my class schedule changed, I decided to find a new job that had the potential for me to earn more money and offered more flexible hours. I quit the pool and the bank and began working as a server at Carino's. To me, Carino's qualified as a "fancy" restaurant, and the servers made decent tips. I was nineteen, tall, thin, cute enough (I thought), and really good at my job.

All of the managers were friendly, but there was one that caught my eye. His name was Jason. He usually managed the kitchen and we sometimes chatted as I picked up the trays of food to be delivered to tables. He had cinnamon skin, dark sultry eyes, and a slow, sexy smile. Six-foot-four, with thick black hair, he looked like he belonged on the cover of a romance novel. He was good-looking, but it was his other qualities that really drew me in.

One night as I was waiting for him to finish arranging the tray, I heard him humming a song from one of my favorite Disney movies. "Wait! That's from *The Lion King*!" I said, giving him a curious look.

"Yup," he winked and handed me the tray, softly singing the romantic chorus as he held my eyes. I turned away, smiling to myself, a little thrill zinging up my spine.

I had been working there for a few months when another manager brought in a large sheet cake with the words "Happy Birthday, Jason!" written on it. Before the lunch shift started, all the staff gathered in the kitchen to celebrate. I didn't have a chance to talk with Jason then, but as the restaurant began to fill with the lunch crowd, I was able to start our usual friendly and flirty conversations while picking up trays for service.

"Happy birthday," I said as I came up behind him on the expo line. He jumped, then laughed and smiled as he turned to look at me. "So, how old are you now?" I asked coyly, genuinely curious since he had a young, boyish face but was also a restaurant manager.

He eyed me, then shyly and quietly spoke into my ear, "Twenty-nine."

"Twenty-nine?" I repeated, a little surprised. He nodded. "Cool," I said, trying to *act* cool, but my mind and my stomach were doing cartwheels, reeling with this newly uncovered piece of knowledge.

He was older than me—ten years older than me, in fact—but I'd always been told I was mature for my age. Maybe the age difference wasn't really that big of a deal. Oh, what was I thinking? He'd never go for me; I was probably just a kid to him. But a little daydreaming never hurt anyone, right?

The next time I went into the kitchen, Jason slipped a piece of small, folded-up paper onto the tray, catching my eye as he did. I nonchalantly tucked it into my pocket, unable to think about anything else until I could sneak away and read it. When I finally got the chance, I slipped into the bathroom and drew it out of my apron. On it, he'd written the lyrics from a Josh Groban song. Josh Groban, I knew, sang beautiful soaring ballads, although I didn't know which song these particular words had come from. As I read the romantic lyrics over again, my heart swooned.

One night a couple weeks later, my shift was going as normal, with me cycling through the server station and the kitchen, doing my best to be quick and efficient so I could earn the highest tips. Every time I stepped up to the kitchen counter, Jason was there, and he sang softly to me as I waited for the food to be plated. I felt silly even thinking the old-fashioned words, but it seemed like I was being *courted*. *Wooed*. My body tingled under his attention, my mind became all-consumed with thoughts of him. With a sexy smile, Jason slid the food trays over to me. I served my tables as quickly as I could so that I could rush back to spend more time with him. Toward the end of the night, as I approached once more, he looked up at me and slipped a tiny piece of paper under a plate. Anyone else would just think it a ticket stub or a torn receipt. This was our little secret.

I served my table, removed the note, and hurried to a quiet, empty corner to open it. I gasped. It was his phone number. *His phone number.* He wanted to talk to me outside of work! Maybe even *see* me outside of work! He liked me! He really liked me! I couldn't stop smiling. I was on cloud nine, beaming from ear to ear. When I saw him again, his smile matched my own.

He was an adult, with a good job and his own apartment. Granted, he was also my boss, but that just made the possibility of our relationship feel even more romantic and special.

We were two clandestine lovers, trying to find a way to be together. It felt very grown up and a little rebellious, especially given my dad's conservative Christian views on sex, dating, and marriage. But in the past, I had dated boys my own age and I just didn't fully connect or relate to them in the end. *This* would be different. Jason was a *man*, and I was now a *woman*. He found me attractive and beautiful. Sexy. And I *felt* attractive and beautiful and sexy when I was with him. Under his gaze, my body came to life. It was a new, delicious feeling to be proud of my body again, instead of wishing it would disappear.

As I closed out my tabs for the night, and waved goodbye to Jason, I counted the minutes until the end of his shift. When I was sure that he would be done, I took a deep breath and dialed his number. Initially, we were both awkward, unsure of what to say and who should talk first. He finally asked me if I knew the song that the lyrics were from, as he had been passing me notes with single lines from the song over the past couple of weeks. He played the song for me from his end, and as he sang softly along with it, every cell in my body lit up like a firework. We talked about the music we liked and shared our favorite songs, our conversation evolving seamlessly, late into the night. Before we ended the call, he asked when he could see me outside of work, and my body said it couldn't be soon enough.

———

At first, we couldn't hang out at Jason's place because two other Carino's employees lived in the same apartment complex, and Jason and I were afraid one of us would get fired if anyone found out about us. Instead, Jason picked me up in his red Chevy truck and we drove around for hours, talking. Sometimes he serenaded me with love songs, gazing at me seductively as if I was the woman the lyrics had been written for. When the words flowed from his lips, I felt like he was speaking them straight into my heart.

Of course, driving had its limitations. We couldn't look at each other for long or touch each other, aside from holding hands. So one night, we pulled into a parking lot at a nature trailhead. Sitting there in the dark, with Josh Groban playing in the background, we shared our first kiss. He pulled me into his arms, his lips telling me how he felt—that I was not the only one falling hard or who wanted more.

The intensity of our attraction engulfed us. Nothing else in the world existed as we kissed. His hands slid under my shirt and I arched against him, aching for his touch. We jolted apart when someone knocked on the window.

We had successfully evaded our coworkers, but we did not evade the police.

I looked at Jason with wide eyes. Surely, this must be a joke, right? I was so annoyed. I quickly fixed my shirt and rolled down the window. Lights blinded me as the officer shone his flashlight in my face.

"Sorry to interrupt things, ma'am, but I need to see your ID." His eyes flitted back and forth between me and Jason. I reached into my purse and took out my wallet. Another officer came to Jason's side and Jason handed over his license too.

Jason turned to me, and I raised my eyebrows and shrugged, wondering what was going to happen next. We weren't doing anything wrong. Surely, adults did this sort of thing all the time. Making out wasn't a crime.

The two officers came together beside my window. Each held our respective IDs, and they silently conferred on something. I shivered, suddenly feeling ready to leave. The officers split up again to question us individually.

"Ma'am, are you here on your own accord? Are you hurt? Did he do anything to upset you? How do you know him? Are you aware of his age? Do you need any help?" The quiet inquiries came one after the other, and I answered quickly, confused about why they would even ask. Yes, I wanted to be there with him. Yes, I knew how old he was. No, I didn't need help. Jason was responding to questions, too, but I couldn't hear what he was being asked.

With a warning glance at Jason, they handed us back our licenses and left. We left, too, a little embarrassed. As we drove away, Jason turned the radio back on and took my hand. Maybe our little parking lot rendezvous was over, but the night wasn't.

COMPROMISE

2004

t was now January, and having been together for about five months, we decided that the risk of being found out was worth it. We started hanging out at Jason's apartment, no longer caring whether our coworkers saw us. Spending time at his place meant we had even more opportunity to be alone. Jason had been very respectful and had never pressured me to go further than we already had, physically. I hadn't even seen the inside of his bedroom yet. But that evening, we fell asleep on the couch watching TV and then, in the middle of the night, moved upstairs.

The following morning, I woke up to find myself in his king-sized bed . . . surrounded by mirrors. I turned my head slowly, my eyes taking in the dresser with three huge mirrors, a smaller dresser with a mirror, his two nightstands with mirrors, mirrored closet doors, and the mirrored headboard behind me. Sunshine streamed in through a large bay window, sending rainbows cascading across the room as the rays of light bounced off all the glass. I looked over at Jason, who was still asleep. The mirrors were a strange surprise, yes, but I couldn't deny my heart. I was in love with him. I loved feeling loved by him, being wanted by him. I craved it. I was hungry for more of him.

The last few times we met up, I had said I wanted to wait. But I didn't want to wait anymore. I loved him. He loved me. This was the next step. This would take our relationship to the next level. I wanted to be his. I snuggled closer to him, my body longing for his touch. He shifted, drawing me toward him, like he had heard my thoughts.

My hands told him what I wanted and we moved through our foreplay quickly. It wasn't long before he covered my body with his and entered me gently. I cried out. He paused and then moved slowly against me, allowing the pain to ease. After a few minutes, in one smooth motion, he rolled me on top of him.

I was straddling him, sitting up, and, suddenly, all I could see, *everywhere*, were reflections of my body on his. I looked around and saw myself—us—reflected in every single mirror. Jason caught my eye and smiled his sexy half-smile at me. He began to move my hips and I watched our sex scene play out around the room. He kept his head turned, watching us, too, which made me feel uncomfortable. I was amplified from every angle. The whole experience felt like I was watching myself in high definition, like I was being filmed. It suddenly felt important that I perform well, be extra sexy. I leaned down, arching my back and sweeping my hair across his chest, bringing his attention back to me. Kissing him, I focused on his hands, his mouth, him moving inside of me, until I forgot about everything else.

When he finished, I arranged myself to lie next to him so we could cuddle, but he abruptly got up from the bed and headed to the bathroom, leaving the door open. I watched him disappear inside, startled by his sudden departure. *Was everything okay?* I curled up under the blanket and waited for him to come back.

A minute passed, then he called from the bathroom, "I thought you said this was your first time."

I sat up slowly, stunned and confused by his comment. "It was," I replied, my voice betraying my utter shock that he doubted me.

"You didn't bleed," he said, matter-of-factly.

I didn't know what to say to that. I wasn't really in control of whether or not I bled when we had sex. This was definitely my first time. I couldn't understand why he didn't believe me. Had I done something wrong? Had the sex not been good enough?

He came out of the bathroom and began getting dressed for work. "Where are you going?" I asked, hating the panic I heard in my voice. "I thought you didn't have to be at work until eleven." He barely looked at me as he sat on the bed to put on his shoes. When he stood up and it was clear he was really leaving, I started to cry. "Please. Don't go."

He came over to me, then kissed my forehead and said he had to get an early start at the restaurant. "Why are you crying?" he asked. "You don't need to be upset. I'll call you when I get off work."

I heard his footsteps heavy on the stairs; heard him get his keys, and open and close the front door. I remained tucked under the covers, frozen in place, trying to figure out what had just happened. I had expected to feel a flood of love and connection, but instead I was left alone on the bed, naked and vulnerable, wondering if I had done something wrong. I crawled out of bed and searched through the bathroom for a washcloth. I turned on the hot water in the shower, letting it run to scalding, and then stepped in and scrubbed myself from head to toe. My pelvis was sore, and I had to wipe very gently between my legs. I felt filthy. I felt used. Sobs racked my body. Had this even meant *anything* to him? Did he still want me? Would he come back? I had thought my first time would be so magical, so special. Was this how sex was? Was this how love was? Was I overreacting like he'd said? I couldn't answer any of my own questions, so I just let the tears come.

Eventually, I washed my face and got dressed. No way in hell was I going back to my dad's house after this, and I still didn't feel like I could show up at my mom's place unannounced, so I drove to the campus Starbucks to wait until my classes started. The minutes dragged into hours. I tried to keep my mind off of him: *Just drink your tea, review your homework*, I told myself. *Attend your class, answer the professor's questions, ignore the ache in your thighs, pretend your life isn't falling apart. You can do this.*

Jason called me when he got off work. "How was your day?" he asked. He sounded normal, like nothing between us had changed.

How was my day? I repeated in my mind, a bit taken aback by the casual question. For a second, I considered how I might answer: *Well, Jason, thanks so much for asking. Let me see . . . I had sex for the first time; then you made me feel like shit because I didn't bleed; then you left me alone in your apartment; then I spent the next eight hours wondering what the hell I'd done wrong; then I felt mad at myself for wanting to go back to you even though you made me feel like crap; and then you called and I felt ashamed and a little ridiculous because, despite everything, I was so relieved and so glad when I finally saw your name light up on my phone.*

But I didn't say any of that. Just hearing the smile in his voice melted all those thoughts away. "My day was pretty good!" I exclaimed, hope rising inside me.

"Do you want to come over?"

"Sure! That would be great! I'll be there in a bit," I said, though I did feel somewhat conflicted about it. Of course I wanted to come over. I was dying to be with him again, to make sure things were okay between us. But I was also a little disappointed with how willing I was to return to someone who had hurt me like he had. I didn't like feeling so needy and desperate, yet I was helpless to stop it.

When I arrived, he greeted me with an enveloping hug and a soft kiss on the top of my head. A wave of relief washed over me. He wasn't mad. Things were okay. We were fine. I could breathe again. He took my hand and led me to the couch then disappeared for a moment to the kitchen. He triumphantly returned with dinner from the restaurant and surprised me with my favorite dessert. While we feasted and watched TV, his eyes kept meeting mine, making me melt. Folding me up into his arms after dinner, he ran his fingers through my hair while we watched a movie and snuggled.

This time, when we had sex it felt more like making love, and he held me close after. When "I love you" fell out of my mouth, there was no hesitation as he returned the words. At that moment, I felt completely cherished and loved. Everything else I had been so worried and concerned about faded away. Hearing him say that he loved me made me finally believe that it was true. I didn't have to guess or wonder anymore. I felt free, and the freedom that came with the knowledge of his love was invigorating! As long as he loved me, I could conquer the world, do anything, be anything. Having this sudden, new confidence in his love empowered and emboldened me in a way I'd never experienced before. Because I was loved by this man, life seemed ripe with possibility.

As I fell asleep, I had a weird flashback to sitting in the coffee shop earlier that afternoon. Had this day been a nightmare or a fairy tale? I wasn't sure, but it was ending with me safe in Jason's arms, with his words of love pulsing through me like a heartbeat, and that was all that mattered.

———

Being loved by Jason felt amazing, but I soon learned that he was kind of hard to figure out. Although he had been chatty and flirtatious while he was courting me, he was, in truth, very quiet. I had to get used to his silence and feeling ignored when he wasn't in the mood for intimacy. When we arrived at his place after work, having both been bombarded with the chaos and verbal onslaught of the restaurant, I could understand why he just wanted to relax and not talk. But there was so much that I wanted to share with him! Talking with him brought back those memories of how my mom and I used to talk. Like our words swirled around us, creating warm bonds of connection. Talking with Jason made me feel seen and loved. I wanted us to talk about our day and our feelings and our future together, maybe even start talking about me moving in with him, but he was such an introvert and easily annoyed by my chattiness. I rarely got what I wanted, but, really, I couldn't complain. Every so often, we went out and he talked to me about everything under the sun. Or we'd sit on the couch and he would nuzzle me, wrapping me in his arms for a passionate kiss before we made love.

This was my first relationship as an adult, and I knew that love sometimes meant compromise, so I thought what we had was good. The lonely waiting, then the loving, warm embrace. This ebb and flow was uncomfortable and hard sometimes, but the security and love I felt when I was with Jason was so much better than the fear and unpredictability I had experienced living with my dad. My relationship with Jason wasn't always full of joy, but neither was it always full of pain. Based on what little I knew about how the world worked, this felt beautifully, reassuringly normal.

But—if I was being honest with myself—I wanted more.

When Jason was sweet and loving and romantic, it was like all the empty spaces in me were filled up to overflowing; like he was pouring into me the very thing I didn't even know I'd been longing for. I couldn't get enough of him. When he turned on those Josh Groban ballads and sang his heart out to me, tenderly caressing my hand and gazing warmly into my eyes, I felt like the center of his world. I lived for those moments when I was surrounded by his soaring lyrics of love and could feel the strength of his body next to mine, smell his cologne as I leaned into him. It was so easy to believe that I was the only one he had ever loved. Then, when he inevitably withdrew into himself again, the loss of his attention left me craving more. I was an addict—willing to do whatever it took to make him happy, if he would give me just one more hit of his affection.

I quickly realized that, while music and romance were my love language, Jason's love language was football and movies. Those were his favorite things to do on his days off, so I found myself watching a lot of ESPN *SportsCenter*. In the beginning, I was bored and wished we could do something else. I soon accepted that if I really wanted to interact and engage with him, I needed to participate in the things he enjoyed. Besides, that felt like the grown-up and mature thing to do. I could join my boyfriend in his excitement for the game, or analyze a quarterback's decision, or cry out in frustration when his team lost. I always loved getting texts from Jason, and it was obvious that I got more texts from him when we messaged about football.

I began watching the games with him, studying them like he did. If Jason and I were apart and I had access to a TV or someone who was keeping tabs on the game, I would get as much information as I could so that Jason and I could discuss it when we were together again later. I learned all of the players' and coaches' names, and chose to cheer on—or despise—the same teams Jason did.

I listened to the ESPN commentary and shared my own thoughts about the games. That zing of satisfaction zipped through me whenever Jason agreed with my analysis or looked at me, impressed with how much I knew. His eyes lit up as we talked, and when we shared high fives after a good play, or celebrated a touchdown, the love between us seemed to increase tenfold. The bond that we were developing felt strong and important and real. I wasn't just his girlfriend. We were truly *partners*, sharing our lives and interests with each other.

However, there were still some limits.

I was spending nearly every night with Jason, but I wasn't technically "living" with him. All of my stuff was still at my dad's house. Any time I was there, I avoided my dad or left quickly and lied about where I was going and who I was hanging out with. Any relationship my dad and I still had was tenuous, at best. I wanted nothing to do with him. But I really wanted my mom to meet Jason. At first, I wasn't sure how she would feel about our age gap. But since we had been dating for six months, it felt wrong to keep hiding this huge part of my life from her. When I told her about Jason, and that he was twenty-nine, she raised her eyebrows and gave me a look, then asked me to tell her more about him.

Next, I broached the subject with Jason. "Hey, babe," I said one afternoon when we were hanging out watching TV. "My mom invited us over for dinner so she can meet you. I know you have Friday off, so I figured that would work." I didn't even word it as a question because I was so sure that he would go. Why wouldn't he?

He ran his fingers through his hair, visibly unsure about what to say, then got up and walked into his kitchen. He busied himself getting his classic snack of soda and chips then came back to the couch. "I don't know, sweetie. I only have one day off this week and I work the morning shift on Saturday." I sat beside him, speechless. "And, you know me," he continued, "I really don't like hanging out with other people. I like to relax and just stay at home—with you." He put his hand on my knee and squeezed it. "I don't even like hanging out with my own family," he finished with a short laugh.

I knew this about him, of course, but it still stung. "I just thought . . . I just thought you could meet my mom," I said. "I'd really love for you to meet her."

I could sense his final answer before he said it. "Sorry, babe. No." He saw the disappointment on my face and rubbed my leg. "Maybe another time."

I sat there, pouting on the couch. He reached for the remote and turned up the volume on the TV. As he began eating his snack, I could see that our conversation was over. I was so bummed. I really hadn't thought he would say no. I tried to understand his reasons, knowing they were valid: He had a busy week ahead. He wanted to relax. He didn't want to stay out late at my mom's and then wake up early for work on Saturday. As I mentally evaluated his response, I slowly started to believe that maybe he was right; maybe another time *would* be better.

I went to my mom's house for dinner that Friday, feeling nervous, like it was a risky move. I didn't want to disappoint my mom or not spend time with her, but I also didn't want to leave Jason when we could be spending the night together. I went to her house early, figuring that I could eat dinner there and then return to be with him for the rest of the evening.

"Hey, honey!" my mom said, greeting me with a hug as I entered her apartment. "Oh, where's Jason?" she asked, seeing I had come alone.

"Um, he's so tired from work, he just didn't feel up to it tonight. But he said thanks for the invite and that he'd love to come another time," I explained. She nodded.

Work and fatigue soon became his excuses for everything. He repeated them over and over and over, and I believed him every time. I mean, it made sense. Some people weren't social, and I knew he got worn out from a long day of putting out managerial fires and navigating other people's demands.

Over time, disappointment became a familiar feeling, and it no longer bothered me as much as it had at first. After a year of consistently inviting him to join me at family events, I finally stopped asking. "Becca!" he had said loudly one night, exasperated with yet another request. "I've told you no. This family stuff just isn't my thing. I don't want to go. If you want to go, that's fine, I don't care, but stop asking me about it." I could tell by the set of his jaw and the tightness in his shoulders that he was frustrated with me. I didn't want to upset him. I didn't want to lose him over something so stupid as inviting him to dinner out with the family to celebrate my sister's birthday or even driving around to look at holiday lights with my mom.

I crept over to where he sat on the couch, unsure how he would receive me. "I'm sorry," I said softly as I tucked myself under his arm.

"It's okay," he said, hugging me, not taking his eyes off the TV. "Don't worry about it."

Being with him took precedence over everything else. I avoided group projects in my college classes because I knew they would take up extra time away from him. I left right after work, instead of hanging out with the other servers. "I'm so tired," I would say. "I have a ton of homework!" Shoulders drooping, eyes heavy, I rejected any offers to go out to eat or go dancing or go to a party. I'd feign yawns and walk slowly out to my car, only to rush over to Jason's apartment from there.

He never got angry with me if I didn't come over or told me that I needed to be with him. Sometimes, when I showed up, he was engrossed in a TV show or even passed out on the couch and barely knew I was there. But being with him made me feel loved and wanted. And wasn't this how relationships worked? You spent all the time you could with the other person, showing them how loyal and committed you were. I thought this was what love looked like.

––––––––

As that year with Jason came to a close, my doctor told me I needed to have surgery. The female issues I'd exhibited in childhood had continued, despite my having been placed on birth control at age twelve to "solve" them all. Obviously, Jason knew what I'd been dealing with, but I could feel him distance himself from me anytime I brought up what surgery and recovery might entail.

As I arrived home after a day of classes and doctor's appointments, I slumped on the couch across from Jason and let out a sigh. "Well, my doctor said she needs to do surgery. She knows what part of the problem is but not all of it, so she needs to go in to resolve it. I'm so tired of being in pain all the time. I'm just ready for whatever it is to be fixed."

"Surgery?" he asked, briefly pulled away from his show.

"Yeah, in a couple weeks at the beginning of December. Depending on how it all goes, I'll definitely have to take it easy and recover."

Turning back to the TV, he replied, "Oh, okay. So are you gonna stay with your mom then?"

I had hoped that Jason would offer to take time off of work to care for me. There was no question that I would have done so for him. But he hadn't even asked about what I would need or suggested that I stay with him. He made it sound like the best thing for me was to be with my mom, even if I didn't agree. My mom, too, was surprised that I wasn't going to stay at Jason's. However, when I told her that his schedule was so chaotic and unpredictable, he simply couldn't do it, she seemed to understand. I hated the idea of being a burden to either of them, but I could see that it made more sense to stay with my mom. She would be much more attuned to what I might need and better able to help with her less-intensive work schedule.

My mom had witnessed my struggles, and despite the fact that our relationship was still a little shaky, she was the obvious choice to help me post-surgery. She knew that staying at my dad's house was not an option, since she had seen how mean and unpredictable his behavior had been around me and my sister, and she understood that I didn't want anything to do with him. Although I had still never told her about the persistent bathroom and shower experiences, what she knew of my dad was bad enough that she never questioned my choice to stay with her.

Our plan was for me to stay at her apartment during the first part of my recovery, even though her couch was the only "bed" she had available. She and my Grams, who was also staying with her, could provide any and all support I might need. This arrangement was hard for me to accept because I didn't want to be away from Jason for that long, and my mom's apartment wasn't my "home" (nor was her couch the most comfortable). This whole situation was a painful reminder that, actually, nowhere was really "home." I didn't have a place where I could truly unpack my things and live. Where I belonged. Jason's apartment was simply where I spent most of my time, and I desperately wanted *him* to be my home.

Staying with my mom for those couple weeks was an incredible help in recovery, but also for our relationship. Of course, we spoke with each other, but more than anything, she *showed* me her love. She helped me get up, eat, take medicine, and lay back down. We went on walks—first incredibly short ones, but then longer ones to help me heal. She made me meals and snacks, helped make sure I had whatever TV shows, movies, or books I wanted to entertain myself. If I needed something in the middle of the night and couldn't get up, she was just a shout away and not once did she bat an eye at any request. I felt like her little girl again. I always was, I guess, always will be—but I hadn't *felt* that way in a long time. She took care of me, and not until she felt I was really ready did she give the motherly "okay" for me to return to Jason's apartment.

Although I now felt more welcome and at home in my mom's space, I was thrilled to get back to Jason. I had been calling and texting with him while at my mom's and he seemed excited to see me as well, though he was always too busy to stop by for a visit. We arranged for him to come pick me up since my car was still over at his complex. It didn't really occur to me that this would be the first time he met my mom until he was standing at her door. As I opened it slowly and let him in to help me with a few things, my mom came around the corner of her kitchen. She introduced herself and held out her hand, which he promptly took and threw on his megawatt smile. They exchanged pleasantries and then my mom ran me through a few reminders before we headed out. They both had that nervous energy that sometimes comes when meeting someone new, but they both had been smiling when we left, so I chalked it up as a success.

A few months later, I wanted to take my mom out to dinner to thank her for everything she had done for me. I asked Jason if he wanted to come. "Not really. I mean, I've already met her," he replied. Then he seemed to notice the disappointment on my face. "Well, you know what? Why don't you bring her to the restaurant? Maybe if I can get away for a minute, I'll stop by and say hi."

Taking my mom to the restaurant where we worked wasn't exactly what I had envisioned for our special night, but it *did* solve the problem of having them both there for the occasion. It would allow me, in a way, to spend the evening with Jason and my mom, together, so I said yes.

ENOUGH IS ENOUGH

2005

J ason and I had now been together for a little over a year. We had fallen into a blissfully mundane routine of me still working as much as I could while going to school full time and Jason advancing in his career as a restaurant manager. The subject of marriage came up every once in a while, but honestly, Jason and I were so busy it didn't feel like we had time to really consider it. Besides, we were happy with how things were. I felt secure and confident in our relationship and I was pretty sure he felt the same.

Over time, Jason had become accustomed to seeing my things in his apartment. Even though he balked at me formally "moving in," I noticed that if I slowly added to my supplies, he either didn't notice or just didn't say anything. I could add clothes to the drawers I was already using, put some products in the shower or have my toothbrush on the counter as long as I did so without any fanfare. If I were to do the same exact things but announce them, that would have been too official for him, and he would have said no.

I brought over more clothes as I gathered them from my dad's house, and when I bought something new, I brought it "home" with me to his apartment. I even put a few items in his closet on the side he was not using, and eventually, my items took up about five feet of hanging space. He was putting his dry-cleaned work shirts away one day while I was getting dressed for work. He opened the closet door and paused. "I see you have some things in here," he said. I held my breath in fear of what was to come next. I didn't know if I could handle hearing that I wasn't welcome in his space and he didn't want my things there.

"Yeah, just a few things," I nervously replied.

"Well, I'm not using this side, so if you need it, it's okay."

My whole body sagged with relief. It wasn't permission to move in all the way, but it also wasn't being kicked out. His acceptance of my clothing there felt like a small step toward officially sharing space together, and it made me feel as if his love for me was growing.

———

I was trying to juggle a full schedule at the local community college, following the prescribed path of classes to later transfer into the architectural engineering program at a state university. The more I learned about the field, though, the less and less I enjoyed my classes. I'd always excelled in school, so at first I was confused why this felt different and so much harder. My classes were not very interesting, were incredibly challenging, and I didn't understand how some of them related to the degree I was pursuing. I obviously didn't know *all* the details of the engineering program, but advanced chemistry and calculus II seemed more trouble than they were worth. After my surgery, I'd had to take a lot of time off and had all that time to think about what I was doing in school. Having that time away from my classes and to reflect on my life, I started to think that maybe I didn't really want to be pursuing this engineering path. After all, I was only doing it because *my dad* had said it was a good idea.

Sitting in the library one day, studying chemical bonds, I realized—this degree was supposed to be for *me*. Yet, I was on track to get the degree and education my *dad* had wanted me to get. I was not doing this for myself—and that no longer made any sense. Why would I work so hard for *my dad's* idea of success? It seemed so ridiculous once I thought about it. But, if not engineering (or interior design), then what could I do that would provide a good, stable, reliable income?

A few weeks later, I was donating blood for the campus blood drive when it came to me: I could be a teacher. I'd had so many teachers throughout the years who had made me love school and provided a refuge when I needed hope and positivity. Now, I could be that teacher who inspired her students and made learning fun! Inside, my heart leaped up in answer with an enthusiasm I hadn't felt in a while. After I recovered from the blood donation, I immediately went to the library and began researching universities that had established teaching programs. I couldn't believe it when I saw that a new satellite campus had opened near me with an elementary education option. I wouldn't have to move out of town or pay to live on campus. Almost nothing about my current situation would have to change, but I could start investing my time and energy into a career that actually excited me.

By the end of spring semester, I had applied to the university, been accepted into the elementary ed program, and miraculously, *all* of my seventy-two credit hours from community college had transferred over. *Is this really happening?!* It had gone so smoothly, been so easy, I felt even more reassured that I had made the right decision. Now, I really felt like what I was doing in college was my choice. It was for me and my future, and whomever I chose to share that with—not for anyone else.

―――――

Once I had a solid grasp on my career path, it felt like I was really taking control of my life. There were a few things I still had to wrap up though. I was spending all my time at Jason's apartment, of course, but I still had a fair amount of things at my dad's. I hadn't made a big production of taking my things from my dad's house up to this point; I was just trying to slowly *fade away*. I stopped by the house every so often to get clothes and did so when I knew my dad wasn't there. I knew, with everything in me, that if I was going to move on and have that normal life I desperately wanted, my dad could not be part of it. I thought I could make that happen quietly, just disappear from his world.

Beth had moved out several months before. Her relationship with my dad had come to a head after he called the cops on her for disobeying his very unclear curfew and kicked her out of the house. We didn't talk very much, but now she was living with her boyfriend and working on figuring out her life too. I was relieved that she had been able to make her escape, although it hadn't been without its difficulties. I hoped to avoid such a confrontation with my dad if I could, but one afternoon, when I stopped by to grab some supplies, my dad was there, and he immediately began accusing me.

"Oh, hello there, stranger," he said with a sneer. "Haven't seen you around lately. Where have you been?" His tone was anything but friendly.

"Well, hi to you too, Dad. For your information, I've been staying at a friend's house." I tried to keep walking to my room, but his body blocked me from going beyond the kitchen.

"I'm done with your lies, Becca. Tell me the truth. Where have you been?" The directness of his words felt like a slap across my face.

"I told you, I'm staying with a friend," I replied, not bothering to disguise my annoyance at being questioned.

"Now, come on, Becca," he said, taking a step closer to me, "I don't think that's true." I recognized that steely, contemptuous tone, the barely contained anger beneath it. He crossed his arms over his chest and lifted his chin, threatening. "I think you've been staying with someone else. I know you've been sleeping somewhere else for a while now." He gave me a knowing look, his eyes hard and condemning.

Well, shit. I had hoped that my absence hadn't really been noticed. He had seemed to be busy and distracted with work and his new girlfriend, and with my schedule I was never home when he was. Was it wishful thinking to hope that he had forgotten about me? Instead, he had become suspicious.

I had to think and act fast. He wanted an answer, but telling him about Jason might result in his raging and thinking of ways to punish me. No way in hell was he going to remain calm if I told him I had been sleeping over at a man's apartment this whole time, the obvious inference being that we were having sex (which was also absolutely forbidden). *All I have to do is buy myself some time*, I thought. Over the years, I had learned that the safest way to placate him in times like this was to offer up a simple lie with a splash of truth in it.

"If you really want to know, Dad, sometimes I stay with Mom. And these last few months, I've stayed with a friend from work," I answered, letting the tone of my voice match his. "She's going through a pretty bad breakup and needs some support. Now, I need to hurry so I can get to work." I stepped around him and calmly walked down the hallway to my room, my heart pounding in my chest. With a decade of experience under my belt by this stage, I knew the best strategies to avoid or disengage with my dad. Unfortunately, I almost always had to lie to do it.

In general, I considered myself an honest person, but I'd become comfortable with lies like this one: easy, insignificant lies to keep my dad off my back. Fudging the truth in order to protect myself was different than just straight-up lying, I thought. And those times I had to lie about how I felt? I didn't consider that self-betrayal as much as self-defense. "Yes, Dad, it's fine." "You're right, Dad, I understand." "I shouldn't have done that, Dad, I'm sorry." No, I hadn't ever been fine or sorry, and I rarely thought he was right, but giving him the submission he wanted had allowed me to escape his clutches more quickly. Either way, when it came to him, lying was a tool I no longer hesitated to use.

Inside my bedroom, I waited a moment, wondering if he had followed me. Would I have to defend myself again? Holding my breath, I listened for footsteps. Not hearing anything, I quickly gathered what I needed, took a last look around my room, and slipped back into the hall. I wanted to leave before things escalated.

I walked quickly to the front door and was getting into my car when my dad appeared in the doorway. "Becca! Come back here! I want to talk to you!" I started the car and backed out of the driveway, pretending I hadn't heard him.

I wasn't even five minutes down the road when he called my cell phone. I felt that old warrior suddenly rise up within me, and knew instinctively that this was it: *The final battle*. Take no prisoners. Don't back down. Fight to the death. I needed to make my stand so clear that there would be no room for misinterpretation.

I didn't let him say a word before I launched into him. "I don't want you in my life anymore! I don't want to see you or hear from you ever again! I don't want anything to do with you, other than for you to leave me alone! I'm done. *I'm done*. I'M DONE!" I immediately hung up, crying and shaking. It hurt to say those words, even though it was a decision that had been a long time coming.

For some, to lose the most important man in their life would be a tragedy. But, after all the pain and confusion and shame he had caused me, I felt like I was saving my own life by cutting my dad off. To that point, he was no longer my *dad*. I couldn't change or deny the fact that he was my biological father, but I refused to think of him as dad anymore. "Dad" signified love, caring, smiles, and hugs. "Dad" felt like someone who you loved, who loved you and supported you and made you feel that anything was possible. "Dad" cheered you on and sat beside you and held you when you cried. All my life, I had been hoping for those things with him, but now it was too late. I was done waiting.

Although I was crying, I felt free. I felt like I could see clearly for the first time. It was suddenly obvious how blinded I had been by his lies and manipulation. He gave me his love as long as I did whatever he wanted. But as soon as I was strong and independent, expressing my own thoughts and feelings, he withdrew his affection. To regain control, he tried to break my spirit, force me into submission like an animal into a cage. He was happiest when I felt helpless.

Now, I was free! I could think and do for myself. I could be totally independent, do and be and say and think whatever I wanted.

No one can stop me, I thought, feeling reckless with liberation. *No one can control me anymore.*

TOO LITTLE, TOO LATE

2005

Despite my request for him to leave me alone, after that phone call, my father—who had grown less and less interested in me over the years unless I was in the bathroom—suddenly began pursuing me in odd ways. When I showed up at my mom's house for dinner or for a visit, she would reluctantly hand me random little trinkets that he had dropped off, saying he was *thinking of me*: award ribbons from church or sporting events, or a medal from a track tournament; ceramic Disney figurines of Winnie the Pooh or Tigger that should have had sentimental value to me, but now just seemed like more evidence that he still saw me as a child rather than an adult who could make her own life choices. He must have gone into my room and selected the first thing he could grab, probably hoping to lure me back with these lame reminders of what I had left behind.

Did he think these things would make me feel better? Did he think these useless gifts, my own possessions, would somehow negate all the shit he had put me through? Did he think that his little offerings would tug at my heartstrings and send me running back into his arms? I didn't understand his tactics. He wasn't sending me flowers or cards or purchased gifts, things that *might* have actually felt meaningful. I can't say what, if anything, would have made me reconsider my relationship with him, but it certainly wasn't this. These feeble attempts just showed that he didn't even care about how much he had hurt me or how much his actions and words had affected every aspect of my life.

In fact, I think those stupid gifts made the rift between us even deeper. Each absurd item my mom passed along to me was another piece of evidence that my father just didn't understand the depth of the pain he had caused.

After the blowup with my father, I showed up on Jason's doorstep with my duffel bags stuffed full of clothes. When he opened the door, his face immediately told me that my bags were not welcome. "Uh, I don't think there's any more room in my closet, Becca," he said. He looked down at the bags again, shaking his head slightly, then left the door open as he returned to the couch to continue watching his show.

Well, shit, I thought. *What the hell am I going to do now?* I put two of the bags back in the car and snuck in the few things I needed for that weekend. Standing in front of the closet that night, trying to think about how I could make my things fit, I couldn't help but feel rejected, like maybe Jason didn't *really* want me here at all. I mean, he was right—we were running out of available space—but I thought he would understand that if things with my dad weren't so bad, I wouldn't be in this position. I wanted Jason to recognize the significance of what I had just done, to welcome me and tell me that I belonged there, with *him*.

The following week, I drove to my mom's apartment and asked if I could put some things in her small on-site storage area. As I was unloading my stuff, she handed me an envelope with a check inside of it. "What's this?" I asked, confused.

"It's a check from your father," she said matter-of-factly, rolling her eyes.

My stomach clenched. "I don't want it," I said, handing the envelope back to her. I knew a bribe when I saw one. My father had been sending me text messages and passing *thinking of you*s, and *I hope you're doing okay*s through my mom and my sister. He had told me that he would not pay for my education, so it was rich that he was sending me money *now*. When the third check arrived, my mom tried giving it to me, yet again. I felt bad for her. She was stuck in the middle. Due to the time-sharing arrangement for my younger brother, she still had to interact with and see my father once a week. It was during those meetings that he would ask her, in his sweetest voice I'm sure, to *please pass this on to Becca, and let her know I love her*. Ugh.

"Mom, I've told you. I don't want his money!" Taking anything from him would feel like violating the boundary I had set.

"Becca," she said gently, "sometimes the Lord works in mysterious ways." Smiling slightly, she gave me a pointed look and extended the envelope toward me again. "Cashing the check doesn't mean you owe him anything in return." My mom understood what my father was trying to do because he'd done the same kind of things to her in that brief period of kindness following her suicide attempt.

I thought about it for a minute and understood what she was saying. I did need the money, but I didn't have to submit to his attempts to "buy me back." I could take the money as a gift and leave it at that. It would kind of be like giving him the middle finger, and I liked that idea. Needless to say, the checks stopped coming when he realized I was cashing in on his financial generosity and ignoring everything else.

A few weeks passed, and then my mom told me my father had said I could come get the rest of my stuff from the house. Though I was glad to finally get the opportunity to retrieve everything, it felt like a punishment too. *If Becca won't talk to me, I won't store her crap anymore. If Becca won't do what I want, then she has to get her shit out.* But, at the same time, why did I care? I hated that place—and him—anyway.

My mom said she would come with me to help me pack up my remaining things. Together, we loaded up my dressers, the rest of my clothes, some books, pictures, and all of my knickknacks. When we were done, the pile seemed simultaneously massive and minuscule. Since Jason didn't want me bringing anything more into his apartment, my mom had agreed to let me put everything in her storage unit. We opened the unit up, and I carefully crammed all my things inside, not surprised to see my sister's stuff taking up space too. My poor mom. Having to store all this shit for the two of us while we were, for all other intents and purposes, living somewhere else. It would have made so much more sense to just leave it all at my father's house, like daughters in normal families might do, but he was such an asshole and so controlling that we didn't want to have any reason to go back there ever again. I knew my mom understood, but I still felt bad about it. *I'll make it up to her*, I thought. *I'll come visit her and make sure I spend more time with her to show my appreciation.* Our relationship was so much stronger now, but she had done so much for me already. I didn't want to cause her any more trouble.

————

About two months after I'd picked up my things and fully moved out of his house, my father showed up at the restaurant where I was working. I had left Carino's and started a new server position at Texas Land and Cattle. I had only been there a few weeks when I happened to glance toward the front door just before the dinner rush only to see my father. His brown eyes caught mine and he held my gaze, a triumphant smirk slowly tilting the corners of his mouth. *Gotcha.*

I turned on my heel and fled into the kitchen. How had he known I would be there? My heart was pumping, and annoyance, anger, and fear coursed through me. What was I supposed to do? I couldn't go out to the dining room, knowing he was watching me; those eyes following me around again, assessing me, ogling my body. I didn't know how angry he was about me leaving his house (even though he had practically forced me out) or refusing to accept or properly acknowledge his "gifts." The unpredictability of it all sent a chill down my spine. But I was working, I *had* to go back out there.

I leaned against the wall, taking a second to strategize. I could see the line cooks across from me busily prepping for the evening service, and knew my time was running short. I looked through the server window out into the restaurant and didn't see him near the entrance to the kitchen. Just then, the opposite kitchen door swung open, and the hostess walked in, looked around, and came toward me. "Hey, Becca," she called. "Did you know that your dad is here to see you?" She smiled brightly, like his presence was a good thing. To her, it was no big deal, maybe even a special treat for a parent to drop by. I'm sure my father was up there with his fake smile plastered on and his good guy persona firmly in place. Why was it so easy for him to get everyone on his side?

I knew that I was safe in the kitchen. I didn't think he would make a scene because that would cause others to think poorly of him. No, he would continue to play the sweet, doting father, and I would look like the cruel, selfish daughter.

"Becca? Are you coming? I need to get up to the front," the hostess said as she turned to leave the kitchen.

"Um, no, not yet. I just need a minute," I answered, still unsure what I was going to do. "Please don't seat anyone in my section, okay? I'm not ready yet." As she slipped back into the main room, I could see that the dinner rush was starting, and now I was going to miss out on the night's first tips because my father couldn't respect the boundaries I had set.

As I continued standing there with everyone else bustling around me, I became less scared and more and more annoyed. How dare he continue to interfere with my life! How dare he walk in here and demand to see me like he owned me, like he had the right to talk to me. I was still debating my next step when one of the managers saw me and casually let me know that my dad wanted to speak with me and I'd better hurry because it was getting busy.

"I've asked him to leave me alone," I replied. "I don't want to see him." My manager looked at me, the frustration and confusion clear on his face.

"Becca, I don't have time to deal with this right now," he replied. With his hands on his hips, he looked past me to the other servers and cooks, making sure they were doing *their* jobs and not holding everything up like I was.

My mind raced as I tried to figure out how to convey the situation to him as quickly and succinctly as possible, knowing that all he cared about was that I get back to work.

"I know, I'm sorry. But, please," I begged, "my father is not a safe person. I cannot go out there with him."

My manager huffed and rolled his eyes, then turned and went back out to the dining area. He returned a few minutes later, letting me know that he had asked my father to leave, and that I needed to get out there so they could open up my section.

The whole night, I watched the front door like a hawk. I felt hypervigilant, sure that my father would not be so easily deterred. I was so distracted during my shift that I found it difficult to take orders when all I could think about was that this was how it would be now: him showing up unexpectedly, me trying to hold the line I had drawn. But then again, he had never respected my requests before, so why would he start now? I tried reassuring myself, reminding myself that I was brave, that I could handle this, handle him.

As the restaurant closed up, I asked some of the other servers if they would walk out to my car with me. I was so nervous to approach them, but I was more scared that my father would be waiting for me in the parking lot. In response, some of them asked if I was okay. I think they had seen how shaken I was about my father showing up. No, I wasn't okay, but I didn't want to open up that can of worms. "I'm fine," I told them. "It was just a weird night."

After we got near my car, I waved goodbye and thanked them. I settled myself inside my car and closed the door. I sat there for a minute, imagining what my coworkers must be thinking about me. *God, what a bitch. Who refuses to talk to their dad?* But was I being a bitch? Kind of? Maybe? I didn't know. I did know that I didn't like being mean. I didn't like being aggressive or demanding. That's not who I was. But I was just doing my best to hold the new rules I'd set. I didn't know what else to do. This was all new to me. Had I been in the wrong? Should I have just sucked it up and talked to him?

Instead of feeling strong, I now felt dumb and embarrassed that I'd had to inconvenience everyone else. In maintaining my boundary with my father, I'd become a burden to other people. The hostess was annoyed at me, my manager was frustrated, and customers had been angry that they had to wait because my section wasn't open. I had caused all these problems that other people had to solve, just because I wouldn't talk to my own father.

But it wasn't really my fault! *He* was complicating things. He was showing up out of the blue when I'd asked him to stay away. He sent me texts when I'd said I didn't want to hear from him ever again. He left me voice mails, complaining about what an ungrateful bitch I was, before remembering himself and calling me sweetie and asking me to call him back. He was the reason I now felt like I was constantly looking over my shoulder, wondering what he might ruin next.

Miraculously, after that night, my father ceased all contact with me. I didn't hear from him for years.

2007

It was Thanksgiving. Jason had agreed, for once, to spend the holidays with his family. We sat around the dinner table with his parents doing the usual chitchat about school and work and what we'd been up to. After a while, Jason began talking about how his apartment was so cramped and lacked room for us to move around and fit all our things. His mom chimed in and asked, "Then why don't you just get a house? I don't know what home prices are up where you live, but I bet you could afford one together, especially once Becca graduates." Jason and I gazed wide-eyed at each other, and a smile slowly began to spread across his face.

"No, we hadn't thought of that," he said. "But that could be really nice." Across from him, I nodded, trying to keep my expression neutral and not let everyone see the tingle of excitement and hope erupting within my heart.

His mom added, "There are a ton of new home developments popping up and the prices are reasonable. You should look around when you get back!"

A home. A new home. Just for us. It felt like such a long time coming and also such a dream come true. It would be *ours*. I wouldn't have to feel like I was stealing space from Jason anymore, and I could finally get all my stuff out of my mom's storage unit, and *Ooh!* I could decorate the house however I wanted! To have a place we could call our own and truly make it our home, together, felt like another piece of my life was beginning to fall into place.

We lay in bed in his parents' house that night and quietly spoke into the darkness. "Can we really go look at houses when we get back?" I asked, unsure if I could fully give in to the excitement.

"Yeah," he sighed contently. "I think we can. I didn't think about it before, but it would be really nice for us to have more space. It feels like the next step for us, and I have seen several new developments going in all over town." I smiled even though he couldn't see me. I couldn't help it! I was way too excited and immediately started imagining what our house, *our new home*, would look like. Interrupting my musings, Jason spoke again, "And, I mean, if we're going to get a house, we might as well get married."

"Wait, what? Really?" I quickly rolled toward him and it took everything within me to keep my voice down.

"Yeah, really," he said as he turned toward me. "It would just formalize what we already have." He gave my nose a kiss. "So, maybe you can pick out a ring when we get back too."

2008

Neither of us wanted a big wedding—and we didn't have many friends anyway—so we exchanged our vows that spring in a small, unpretentious ceremony in my mom's backyard with just a few people present. I wore my fanciest dress, even though it was black, and we kissed under a giant oak tree, sealing our commitment forever. I finally felt like our relationship was permanent, a sure thing. Any worries or niggling insecurities fell away, replaced entirely by joy.

That summer, we closed on our new-build house, and I was finally able to move all my things out of my mom's garage. We also bought some new furniture after selling Jason's stuff on Craigslist. I especially loved the warm wood tones, bulky carved headboard, and total absence of mirrors in our new master bedroom set. By then, I had officially quit the restaurant business and earned my teaching degree, and Jason had left Carino's for the senior manager position at the local Italian eatery.

Our lives were *good*. We were so *normal* and happy and boring that going out to the movies—which we did on Jason's days off almost every week—felt like an adventure. Jason knew everything about every actor in every movie, and he rattled off their stats on the way to the show. He was thrilled to get popcorn, candy, and a large soda, his eyes lighting up every time, as if he was in Willy Wonka's factory. I couldn't help but enjoy all of it right along with him. His energy and excitement were contagious. Whenever the actors on the screen shared a love scene or romantic dialogue, Jason nudged my arm or squeezed my hand, which still gave me butterflies. Later, he usually quoted the movie in bed or via text, the thoughtful gesture reminding me of when we first met. Though we had been together for nearly five years at this point, those little moments made me feel like he was still courting me.

Fully ensconced and protected in my job at the school and with Jason at our new house, I rarely thought about my father anymore. Then my mom called me one evening and said she had something to give to me.

"What is it?" I asked, already knowing I was going to reject it outright.

"It's that hot dog maker. The one we had when you girls were little. Remember?"

The hot dog maker. An extraordinary machine that cooked hot dogs to perfection. Of course, I remembered.

Making hot dogs was probably the only time my father was ever really involved in cooking with us. The machine was basically a single-dog steamer, but it seemed magical. We all stood around the counter while my father showed us how to use it: a little water in the bottom, place the hot dog on the special steaming tray above the water, put on the lid and then position the bun face down on the very top of it all so it would steam too. His smile and satisfaction at this process were contagious. I watched the water bubble and steam as the hot dog changed color and expanded. When the timer *dinged*, my father usually served me first. Maybe because I was the oldest, but probably because I was the most excited about it. I was the one who shared in his joy the most, *his Junior*. He placed the steamed bun on my plate and put the hot dog in it, presenting me with a perfectly cooked hot dog every single time. To me, it seemed like a magic trick, and he was The Keeper of the Hot Dog Machine.

When I was around eight, he told me that when I grew up and he passed away, he would leave the hot dog maker to me, like it was a precious family heirloom. He said he knew how much I enjoyed it and wanted me to have it. It would be a gift that I could always remember him by. He told me this before the bathroom visits started.

My mom's voice broke into my thoughts, "He said he knows it was your favorite and he wanted you to have it. If you don't want it, just let me know."

What the fuck? Was he serious? I only cared about the hot dog maker because it had been a way of spending time with him. Those silly moments with him, before everything got weird and awkward and awful, had made me feel so loved. What I had wanted was to be able to continue that normal, loving father-daughter relationship! I didn't care about the stupid machine. If this was his way of apologizing (which, he had never actually done, by the way), then it was too little, too late.

Looking back, the offer of the hot dog maker seems like a bad omen, considering Jason's favorite meal: chili cheese dogs.

I never made chili cheese dogs again. Not since that phone call from Stephanie.

TRUTH AND TORNADOES

FEBRUARY 2009

realized I was control-cleaning as I straightened the pillows on our king-sized bed for the third time. After the week from hell, beginning with Stephanie's phone call, I needed to feel a sense of accomplishment, a modicum of control. Hands on hips, I looked around the room. Sunlight glinted across the cheerful, dusty-blue walls, perfectly setting off the freshly shined walnut furniture and our coordinating navy comforter. I couldn't help but smile as I fluffed another pillow—one of eight—and arranged it *just so* against the others. To me, our room, which I had so carefully designed while we were planning our new house, said *this is a happy home, and happy people sleep in this bed.*

The area we'd chosen was a developing community, which had meant we got to choose certain aesthetics as the house was being built. I still loved interior design, and so getting to select tile and carpet, paint and countertops had felt like a dream come true.

I could see into our backyard from the bedroom window, and saw our dog Bianca chewing on a bone in the grass. We'd been told she was a pit mix, but later discovered she was mixed with Great Dane. She felt a little too big to be in the house all the time, or at least that's what Jason said, so we mostly kept her outside.

Looking around our yard and the immaculate room, I thought, again, about Stephanie and the accusations she had made against Jason; all those things her daughter was saying. Life hadn't felt as fragile as it did right now in quite some time. Despite my confidence and trust in Jason, I still felt raw and uncertain and vulnerable, as if I were holding a fractured object in my hands and if I held it *just the right way*, maybe it wouldn't fall apart.

I scooped a pile of dirty clothes from the floor and headed toward the laundry room. All week, I had distracted myself, refused to let my mind wander down the rabbit hole of the past. As I went through the motions of cleaning up, though, my mind recalled conversations Jason and I had had, the things between us that had been both spoken and unspoken: every look, every touch, every feeling. I couldn't help but analyze our relationship, albeit from the biased perspective that Jason *loved me*. In our quiet, perfect, beautiful house, I could drown out the excessive drama surrounding us, ignore the other side of the story, and discard all of those details that didn't fit my picture of things working out in our favor. I had started the day feeling disconnected and unsure, like I was living someone else's life. Cleaning and reviewing the facts had calmed me.

Making my way into the dining room, I saw that our Disney photos were still there, spread across our table. Growing up as an 80's kid, Disney represented the idea that magical things could happen in your life. I had witnessed that in their movies—I'd seen the princesses do amazing things; beautiful, strong underdogs who succeeded against all odds. As a child, I had internalized those classic truths: no matter what was happening, no matter what obstacles I was facing, if I just kept believing, the dreams in my heart would come true.

My eyes scanned the images, settling on one of me and Jason laughing and posing with Mary Poppins and Winnie the Pooh, two of my favorite characters from childhood. Looking at our smiles, I knew with utter certainty that Jason and I would get through this. No matter what happened, we were going to be okay. I took a deep breath, quickly organized my scrapbooking materials, and resolved to finish the scrapbook after I was done cleaning. I could show Jason my progress when he got home from work that night.

I had just finished wiping down the kitchen counters when my cell phone rang. I saw Jason's name flash on the screen and answered cheerfully, "Hey, babe!" Instantly, I knew something was wrong.

His voice was quiet and raspy and he was whispering frantically. "I'm sorry, Becca . . . I'm sorry—it's true. I did it. I did it, Becca, I did it." He was crying short, labored sobs as he confessed to me.

"Wait, what? What are you talking about?" The words rushed out of my mouth. Then, realization hit: "Are you serious? Wait—what are you saying?"

"I'm sorry, I'm so sorry." There was a pause and I could hear a commotion in the background. I pressed the phone harder against my ear.

"Jason! Talk to me! Jason!"

He didn't respond and I strained to hear what was happening. The restaurant kitchen was all stainless steel and tile and, now, metal banging against metal clashed with raised, angry voices.

"Jason! What's going on?" I shouted, starting to panic. *What was happening? Was he okay?*

"Becca, I have to go! I'm sorry. I have to go . . . I have to—" Jason's voice cut off and the line went dead.

I couldn't breathe. I felt like all of the air had been knocked out of me. The world slowed to a halt as my mind began to process the things he had said.

It's true. I did it.

His words dropped into my mind, like bombs falling from the sky. As they sank into me, I saw the life I had created—this boringly beautiful, normal life—explode into a million pieces. All the memories, the whispered sweet nothings, the hugs, the kisses, the laughs, the smiles, the intimacy, everything we had been was now destroyed. Completely annihilated.

I raised my phone with shaking hands and called my mom. As soon as I heard her voice, I began sobbing and screaming hysterically, "He did it, Mom! He did it! He lied to me! He lied to me! He just told me that it was all true." I vomited out the words and they tasted like poison, toxic bile spewing from my lips. This was not real. This could *not* be real.

She tried to calm me down, to understand what I was saying. But I was hyperventilating. I felt dizzy and nauseous, like I was being turned inside out.

Through my sobs, I heard another sound. Pounding. Someone was pounding on the front door. *Bang! Bang! Bang!* I flinched with each sound. What the hell was going on? Was someone trying to break into my house? My heart raced. Thank God, my mom was on the line with me.

"Becca! Becca, are you there? What's happening?" I heard my mom's worried voice.

"I don't know . . . I don't know who they are . . ."

Keeping the phone to my ear, I silently snuck over to the door and peered through the peephole. Two men in button-down shirts, cowboy hats, and boots were standing there, hands on hips, waiting. Their faces were stern. *Who the fuck are they?!*

I ran back into our bedroom and locked the door as their fists pounded again, the sound reverberating through the silence. I slipped into our closet and closed the doors, tucking myself into a corner. "Oh my god, Mom," I whispered. "There are two men here banging on my door! I don't know what they're doing! What do they want? Why are they here?"

"You need to call 911," my mom said in her stern "mom" voice. "Hang up right now and call 911!"

Hands still trembling, I disconnected from my mom and dialed 911. I explained to the operator that these strange men were at my house and I didn't feel safe, didn't know what to do or why they were here.

"Just stay where you are. I'm sending an officer over there to check it out. Just stay calm and stay on the line with me." I sat there in the dark, clutching my phone for what felt like hours, waiting for the all clear. Finally, the operator spoke again, "Ma'am? Ma'am, it's okay. You don't need to worry. Those strange men at the door are detectives. They need to speak with you. It's okay, they're the police."

———

After the 911 operator informed me that the men at my door were the police, I realized I couldn't avoid them any longer.

I crawled out of my hiding place in the closet, cautiously approached the front door, and opened it. The two men introduced themselves and said they had a warrant to search the premises. Before I could ask any questions, they pushed past me into the house, telling me to sit on the couch. One man stayed with me, ensuring that I didn't get up or touch anything. A crime scene investigation crew started trickling in and, like ants, they had soon invaded the place.

After a while, a different detective approached me, asking me to come sit in the dining room, away from the other activity, and offered to get me a glass of water. My mom had arrived at the house shortly after I ended the 911 call, coming to make sure that I was okay. The police let her in the house now, and she followed us over to the table, reaching out to hold my hand as we took our seats. The detective explained that Jason had been arrested at the restaurant on charges of indecency with a child by sexual contact. The officer laid his file on the table, right on top of my—our—Disney photos, and began stating the allegations:

Jason had sex with Stephanie's daughter.

And at least five other women that the police knew of.

No, not women—*girls*.

Stoically, the officer read out their ages.

Seventeen.

Fifteen.

Sixteen.

Sixteen.

Seventeen.

But all I was hearing was:

He cheated on me.

He cheated on me.

He cheated on me.

He cheated on me.

He cheated on me.

Then, nonchalantly, he asked, "And, how old were you when you met Jason?"

"Nineteen," I said, blankly. The detective nodded, probably jotting down that I was just another one in the line.

He pulled out a notebook from underneath the file and slid it over to me. Picking it up, I found myself staring down at my own handwriting. It was the notebook I'd used to document everything Stephanie and her daughter had said against Jason. My eyes flicked across my notes. This new information the detective had presented seemed to fill in the blank spaces like pieces fitting into a puzzle.

As I looked up at the officer, his eyes softened, and he spoke gently. "Ma'am, this isn't a 'stand-by-your-man' kind of moment. This is a turn-around-and-run-the-other-way moment."

I had remained emotionless, stiff, as the officer read through the file, but the anger within me exploded as the reality of the detective's words hit me.

"*Arrrggghhhh!*" I screamed, ripping off my wedding ring and throwing it across the room. As more cries racked my body, my mom pulled me to her and I fell into her embrace.

Around us, the police finished up their search, then left. The messy house seemed fitting through my swollen, blurry eyes. Over the last couple of hours, a tornado of emotions had swirled inside of me, wreaking havoc, and that havoc was reflected everywhere I looked. I could no longer control what was happening, what was or wasn't true. No matter how much I had tried to hold things together, it was all out of my hands now. My inner world looked like the aftermath of a tornado too. My perfect, normal life was blown to smithereens, but an eerie stillness had settled around me. I had been clinging to

Jason's words since that call from Stephanie. I was clutching onto his promises for dear life, resisting all other possibilities. And now the truth had come out. The horrible pain of Jason's betrayal was offset by a deep release within me. I hadn't realized how much tension my body had been holding. Now that the tornado had hit, I no longer had to fear it.

My mom suggested that I spend the night at her house. Numb and exhausted, I could only nod.

―――――

My phone hadn't rung in thirty-six hours, not since the truth bombs were dropped, so I was shocked when I got a call as I was sitting on my mom's couch. I didn't recognize the number, but an automated voice told me it was from the county jail. Then I heard Jason speaking. Tentatively, he told me that his parents had bailed him out and he wanted to retrieve his things from our house before going to a hotel. His dad would be arriving in town the next day.

After a moment, he asked, "So, can you come pick me up?"

I was stunned by his audacity for a second, but quickly found my voice. "Where's your truck? Why can't you drive there yourself?" *Good job, Becca,* I prided myself. *Don't give in. You shouldn't help him after what he's done to you!*

He explained that his truck had been impounded and he wouldn't be able to get it anytime soon. I closed my eyes as he spoke, wanting to stay strong.

His question lingered in the silence between us, and I felt the weight of it—just the first of many decisions I would need to make in the coming days, weeks, and months.

My stomach churned as I considered my options. I didn't want to give him what he wanted; he didn't deserve that. But

I knew what *I wanted*, and that was answers. I deserved that much.

"Yes. Fine, I'll come. I'll be there in a little bit."

I slunk into the kitchen where my mom was making dinner, knowing that she would not like the decision I had made. I didn't have to say anything. She had heard my end of the phone call and put the pieces together. She just looked at me with a sigh of compassionate disapproval, and then said she would go with me after dinner.

"But shouldn't we—?" I started, reaching for my purse and car keys.

"No," she said, giving me a pointed look. "We will go when *we* are ready. After we've had dinner. He can wait."

———

It was dark when we pulled up to the county jail. Jason was waiting outside. I stopped the car at the curb, unlocked the doors, and waited for him to get into the back seat. I didn't want to look at him, but my body was still finely attuned to his. I caught a hint of his Kenneth Cole Reaction cologne. I loved that smell, but right now it made my head ache.

I put the car in drive and automatically glanced in my rear-view mirror before backing up. At six-foot-four, Jason's face completely blocked my view. Flustered, I checked all my other mirrors and asked my mom if we were clear.

When we got into the house, I stopped in the living room and turned to face him. "You have fifteen minutes to pack your things," I said, with more authority than I felt. He asked if we could talk. I glanced over at my mom, who raised her eyebrows but said nothing. "Yes," I said. "We can talk after you're finished."

While he was in the bedroom, my mom sat next to me on the couch. "Remember your time limits," she said quietly. "But I'll watch it for you. I'll be right here if you need me. Remember, he lied to you before, he may try to do it again." She took both of my hands in hers. "You have done nothing wrong."

I faced her, soaking up the encouraging words. "You are in charge here," she continued, "not him. He only gets to talk to you if you want to talk, okay?"

I tried to think of what questions I would ask first, which questions I wanted answered the most. But when he came out of the room with his packed bags, all my thoughts became jumbled up.

I followed him up the stairs to the second floor, where we could have some privacy but my mom could still hear if I needed her. We sat apart from each other on the sectional couch in the game room.

"First, I want to say I'm sorry," he started. He looked up at me with those soulful dark eyes, and I let him speak. He told me about being arrested at the restaurant, how upsetting it had been for him, and how the police had manhandled him in front of everyone. "It was so embarrassing," he said.

At that point, I interrupted. "What exactly did you do with her?" He knew who I was talking about. The detective had said there had been others, but *she* was the one Jason had specifically lied to me about. *She* was a face and a name and the one I knew for sure he had been with since he had confessed to it on the phone that day he was arrested.

"We had sex."

Boom.

"How many times?"

He paused, thinking. "I . . . I don't know."

"When and where?" I couldn't stop the questions from coming out, even though I wasn't sure I wanted to hear the truth.

"Sometimes when we were working late at the restaurant, and sometimes while you were at work."

Boom.

"Did you have sex with her *here*? *In our bed*?"

"No." He paused. "On the couch downstairs."

Boom.

"Why? Why did you do this?" I hated the begging in my voice, but *this, this was what I really wanted to know.*

"I don't know," he said softly, leaning forward with his head in his hands.

I was stunned by his words. "You don't know? I'm sorry, that's not good enough!" I declared. "That's not gonna work for me." I waited for him to give me a better explanation. My mind was reeling with all the reasons I had come up with to explain why he had cheated on me with her: because she was younger; she was prettier; she was skinnier; she was sexier. I kept forgetting that, being under eighteen, she was *illegal*; that what he had done was not just immoral, but *criminal*. The only thing that mattered was that he had betrayed me—and an extra twist of the knife—with my coworker's daughter. All I could see was my own pain. Everything else was on the periphery, barely registering.

He lifted his head and looked at me. He moved closer and reached out to touch me. "I love you, Becca, and I'm so sorry. I want to be with you. Only you."

"BULLSHIT!" My mom's voice rang out from below, the syllables loud and clear, like gunshots.

Jason's eyes flew up to meet mine and he tried again, more passionately, this time. "No, I mean it. I know we have a lot to work on, but I want to be with you. I want to go back to the way things were. I love you."

"Becca!" Mom called out, a reminder and a warning.

"It's okay, Mom," I called back. "I've got this." I looked at Jason, this man who I had loved for five years, had given my everything to, and felt like I was seeing him clearly for the first time.

I had realized that I was just one of who-knows-how-many. I was just the one who had stuck around the longest, maybe the one who made it the easiest for him to continue his charade. Had he ever been faithful to me? His confessions of love rang hollow. He had only told me the truth because he got caught. And I hadn't even been the one to catch him! I had been blissfully unaware until the truth was handed to me—well, thrown in my face—first by Stephanie, then by the police.

I could not trust him. But, deep down, I also felt like I was at fault. If I had just been better, been good enough, been more attractive and less needy, made him happier, then maybe none of this would have happened.

I could hear my mom jingling my car keys downstairs. I gathered the tiny kernel of strength I had left and said the words I needed to say.

"No. We're done. It's time for you to go."

He nodded solemnly, accepting my decision, and walked back downstairs to gather his belongings.

I took a deep breath. I had one last step tonight: to drop him off.

I could do this.

———

The car was silent as the three of us drove to the hotel. With each minute that passed, I felt myself start to relax a little more. I was almost done. This part of the nightmare, at least, was almost over.

I entered the hotel drop-off area and put the car in park. Staring straight ahead, I waited for him to get out.

"Umm, Becca?" He hesitated. "Uh, they took my wallet and haven't given it back to me yet. Can you use your credit card and ID to check me in?"

I'm sorry—what the FUCK did you just say?

That's what I wanted to say, what I *should* have said.

I didn't look at my mom, I just grabbed my purse, got out of the car and stormed inside.

"Good evening!" the receptionist called out, greeting me warmly. Her smile faded when she saw my angry face. Jason meekly came to stand beside me as I stepped up to the counter and handed her my card. "Room for one, and one night only."

"I hope he's treatin' you right, darlin'," she said cautiously, peering at me over her glasses.

"Just. One. Night," I repeated, not even wanting to give him that much. We stood there, awkwardly waiting for the receptionist to complete the check-in process and finalize the payment. In that moment, I remembered the first time we had stayed at a hotel together, when we first started dating. I had booked a hotel room for us then too. Jason was always doing little romantic things for me, and I had wanted to do something romantic for him.

"Here ya go!" The receptionist's voice jolted me back into the present. She handed me the key and I immediately turned to give it to Jason.

He took the key and picked up his bags again, clearly waiting for me to say something. But what was one supposed to say in a moment like this? I wished I had something snarky or hurtful to hurl at him, but the words wouldn't come.

I wondered how many times I had been devastated by this man. How many times had I let him hurt me in so many little

121

ways, so desperate for his love, and now I knew that I was never that special to him at all, not really.

The fact that he was standing before me now was proof that I had always put him first. He had always been my main priority. My needs and wants were secondary, almost irrelevant. I wanted him to be happy, to feel taken care of, because his happiness was *my* happiness. I made him his favorite meals. I endured countless hours of ESPN. I tried whatever sexual position he wanted to try. I went to see all the movies he was interested in. I found every way I could to please him because it was absolutely devastating to me when he got upset and took his affection away.

And yet, he had been unfaithful to me over and over and over, again and again and again. I was certain that he had never once considered how I might feel to know that he was cheating on me. Never once had he worried about how much it would hurt me to find out. He had even gone out of his way to set me up to look like a big fool when I passionately defended him in front of Stephanie and my mom. Had he ever really loved me? Or was I just the unsuspecting, naive cover for his little game of sleeping with any teenage girl he could find?

I felt like a dirty rag, used and disposable. And he didn't even care.

"Well, goodnight," I said, and walked out the door of the hotel. I got in the car and drove to the nearest parking spot just out of view of the front entrance. My mom held me as sobs rocked through my body again, even though I thought there was nothing left.

ONE STEP AT A TIME

N early two weeks had passed since I had last been in ~~our~~ my house. I had been staying with my mom, unable to comprehend the disaster that was now my life. I was barely eating and hardly talking. I had so much anger and sadness inside, and there wasn't anywhere for it to go, so I sank inward, into it. I was a walking zombie, physically moving through daily tasks and obligations without thinking. Each day, I drove to work with my thoughts spinning, to the point where I often didn't even remember driving there once I'd arrived. I was just going through the motions. There was no soul-searching, I didn't have the capacity for that. I collapsed in on myself.

"Honey," my mom suggested, "maybe it would be good for you to talk to someone, maybe call a friend." But I didn't have any friends now that Jason was gone. Ever since we started dating, my life had quickly become all about him, us. Friends hadn't seemed important when he was everything I wanted. "Well, maybe it would feel good to get back into a normal routine—you know, to be back in your own house, surrounded by your own things." I wanted to get back into a normal routine, but I couldn't stand the thought of being at home, where there were all those reminders of *him*.

Eventually, my mom decided we needed to take action. She asked some of her friends to come over and help me move some furniture. The couches absolutely had to go. I wanted to burn the couches and watch them go up in infidelity smoke. But since I couldn't figure out the logistics of that, we moved them into the garage instead.

After rearranging some furniture that, to my knowledge, had not been tarnished by Jason having sex with other ~~women~~ girls on it, everyone else left and I was alone for the first time since Jason's arrest. The downstairs was still in shambles from the police executing the search warrant, and now it looked even worse since we had moved everything around. With the house suddenly too quiet, I felt the heaviness of it all trying to pull me under. Trying to shake it off, I put on some music and rolled up my sleeves.

The police had been thorough in their search, so much of the cleaning involved putting things away: tidying up the kitchen, re-filing paperwork, hanging up clothes. Pangs of anger and sadness hit me every time I put away something that was his: his favorite cup, the clothes that still smelled like him, his shampoo. And then the questions started spinning in my mind again.

Why had Jason cheated on me? Was I too ugly? Not young enough? Not sexy enough? Maybe if I had been a better wife, he wouldn't have been tempted by anyone else? Maybe if I had done things differently, would he have been faithful? I felt like a failure as I sorted through the remains of our life together. Why hadn't I noticed? His infidelity had been going on for months, if not years, right under my nose! Was I just dumb? What was wrong with me? How could I not have known?

Standing in our closet, surrounded by his smell, I lay down and cried.

I missed him.

Jason had betrayed me and I didn't want him back, but he had been my person. The one who I had given my heart and soul and love to for almost five years. The one who loved me so fully and completely—or at least I had believed. We had built a beautiful life together. We had bought this house together and made it a home; a home that felt so safe and loving, so different from the home I had grown up in. He had sung me love ballads and quoted movie lines to me, showering me with loving, poetic words. He held my hand, opened doors for me and made sure I was protected from cars when we walked through parking lots. He bought me little candies and surprised me. He had gushed over me, romanced me, made me feel the magic of his love, made me believe that someone *could* love me, would love me; that someone would give me the affection and attention I had desperately wanted. I missed cuddling with him and hearing him serenade me. I longed for his warmth, his touch.

It was all so confusing. I didn't want him anywhere near me ever again, and yet I longed to be wrapped in his arms. I had no idea what I was supposed to do now. How did I move forward from here? How would I survive this?

I felt exhausted. The combination of cleaning and the effort I had been exerting to hold myself together while my mom's friends were here had really taken it all out of me. I wanted nothing more than to go to bed, but my stomach began to growl as I lay there. I didn't want to listen to my physical needs right now. I wanted to collapse inside of myself again, pull the blankets over my head, and not think about anything else. But I could feel my hunger, hear the rumbling in my stomach. Fine. Food. I guess that was simple enough. I could get food. I pulled myself off the floor, went into the kitchen, and opened up the fridge. We I had salsa. And chips! Okay, it wasn't the dinner of champions, but, damn, it sounded delicious. I turned on all the lights as I made my way to the living room and the modified couch and TV setup. Jason had never liked to watch *Bones* or *CSI: Miami*, so I felt a little *fuck you* as I ate dinner and watched *my* shows.

A while later, I heard a bark outside, and decided to let Bianca in. Jason hadn't grown up with a dog in the house and had rarely let Bianca spend time with us inside. *Fuck you, Jason*, I thought, again, as I invited her up onto the recliner with me.

But when I decided it was finally time to go to sleep, it hit me: if he had lied to me about everything else, then who's to say that he didn't have sex with other people in our bed? *Yeah, fuck you, Becca!* (Or, well, *not* me, I guess.)

I didn't know what, if anything, was actually *clean* in our house anymore. On one hand, that made it feel impossible to be there, but on the other hand, I didn't want to give up this house that I had designed, that I had helped build and create. I was just going to have to deal with this in bits and pieces. One thing at a time.

From everything I'd been through before, I knew that my mental vision became very narrow when life felt hard. In intense moments, it felt like whatever I was dealing with was so large and the walls it created so high that I could only see the options right in front of me. All I could see were the struggles, the pain, and the hurt, because the situation felt all-consuming. Some might call it tunnel vision, but that feels too focused.

To me, it felt more like drowning. My mind was too clouded by sorrow and self-pity to see clearly. I was swallowed up by the overwhelming feelings of failure and not being enough.

Something was different this time though. While I did feel like I was being crushed by the depth of Jason's infidelity, that quiet defiance that had shown itself years ago was re-awakening and pushing back against the flood of emotions. After experiencing my father's abuse, my mother's near-death, and my own thoughts about suicide, I had become familiar with that sensation of life closing in on me. But now, this new resistance was swelling up deep inside, buoying me up under the weight of my sadness. It fueled my determination to survive. I felt utterly destroyed, and yet, I knew I was going to be okay. I just had to take one step, and then another.

Sheets. I had fresh sheets.

I stripped the bedding, replaced the sheets, and remade the bed. Bianca came in to check on me. I smiled at her sweet eyes and her huge, ninety-pound body. She usually slept in her crate, but *fuck you, Jason*, not tonight. I got under the covers and patted the bed until Bianca settled next to me.

———

"Becca," my mom said one afternoon, a few days later, "have you thought about getting tested for STDs?"

I looked at her blankly. *No.* What with the emotional tornado I had been struggling to survive, *No, Mom, I had not thought of that.*

As though I were still a teenager, she gently explained that, since we didn't know how many partners Jason had actually had—or that *they* had had, in turn—I should get a full STD panel done, just in case. I reluctantly agreed.

The following day, I found myself in the waiting room of an OB-GYN office filled with glowing pregnant women who seemed as happy as clams—probably because their husbands hadn't cheated on them. As I looked around the room, a new feeling snuck up on me: I was absolutely humiliated. There I was—stupid, clueless Becca, planning babies of my own and dreaming of family vacations—while my thirty-four-year-old husband was out screwing a sixteen-year-old. It was so embarrassing. I hung my head and slouched in my seat, wanting to disappear.

When I was called in, I undressed and settled myself on the paper-covered exam table. The doctor smiled kindly at me and asked what I was there for.

"I need to get tested for STDs," I said plainly. This was my life, now. I had to face it.

"Oh, alright then. Easy enough!" she said, writing something on her chart. "How many sexual partners have you had in the last year?"

"One."

She tilted her head and gave me a quizzical look.

"But," I added, "my husband cheated on me with who knows how many people, so I don't really know, technically, how many partners *we've* had."

The doctor was a little taken aback, but all I had done was tell her the truth. It actually felt like a relief to state the facts out loud, and so clearly. No room for misinterpretation. Surprisingly, sharing my secret seemed to lessen the humiliation of it.

After my appointment, I met my mom and Grams for lunch. "Honey," Grams said carefully, "we want to talk to you about your next steps. About getting divorced."

Divorce. The word was heavy, like an anvil dropping down into the middle of our table. It sat there in the middle of us, unwilling to be ignored.

Yes, I had thought about *that*, but only after first agonizing over whether I was going to give Jason another chance and try to repair our relationship. For my mom and Grams, it was cut and dry: no way in hell should Jason be allowed back into my life. But, for me, it wasn't so clear.

I felt desperate to get back to normal and find a way to stop this awful pain. There were times over the last few weeks when it felt like, *Well, duh! You cannot be with him anymore!* But then, when I was lonely and missing him and remembering the good times, I would convince myself that we could work things out. I imagined an entirely new life with him, where we could start over and reconnect. I imagined him coming home and us spending time together, rebuilding our trust, and renewing our vows. In my dream world, it all seemed so easy: one way to get rid of the pain was to just go back to this man who said he loved me, who I had created a life with. I played out this fantasy—I could see it so clearly—totally forgetting that he could possibly be in prison for the next several years. Forgetting that he hadn't just had an affair, but that he was being accused of *committing a crime*. It felt like a real slap in the face every time I remembered those minor details. Like, *well fuck*, there goes *that* plan.

When I had mentioned all this to my mom a few days before, she looked me in the eye and asked, "Becca, do you really think you're ever going to trust that he is being faithful to you? Do you think you'll be able to trust that he won't do this again?"

Hearing my mom voice those concerns out loud made it harder for me to ignore them. I thought about her questions for a while, and my answer was no. I was never going to be able to trust him 100 percent; there was always going to be a niggling doubt in the back of my mind about what he was doing, and where he was. I pictured myself being hypervigilant about who he was spending time with; the employees he talked about—or didn't talk about—the most. I pictured myself checking his email, looking through his texts, interrogating him when he came home a few minutes late. That was not the relationship I wanted; it didn't sound fun and it certainly didn't sound like love. Not to mention that kind of relationship would be very different from the one we'd had (but did I want *that* anymore?). I had to accept that there was no going back.

Divorce was the only option, even though I hated to admit that. I had been raised to believe that, when people love each other, they don't just give up, they work through their problems. I made an exception for my mom, of course, because I knew the hell she had lived through. There was no future for her with my father, just like I had to accept that there was no future for me with Jason—or, probably, anyone else.

It seemed my reality was this: my marriage was over, my life was over. It was all downhill from here. Who else would want me, a twenty-four-year-old woman who wasn't even good enough to keep her husband happy and faithful? I was damaged goods, the bruised apple in the proverbial cart. I had clawed my way out of my father's clutches into what I thought was a normal, healthy, loving relationship. I had done all the things I thought I needed to do to have a great life, and, yet, here I was, cast aside like a piece of garbage by the man I loved. That was all the evidence anyone needed to know that I wasn't worth it.

Letting my life shatter around me and accepting that Jason and I were really, truly over felt like death.

Oh, and the practical side of things? The house, the dog, the finances, the furniture, the splitting up of everything—that felt impossible too.

I remembered hearing the phrase, "We do the best we can until we know better, then we do better." I could see that I had been going down a path, believing it to be beautiful and right, and now I had to accept that my life hadn't been as great as I'd thought it was. When I thought about my relationship with Jason, I could see, in those rare moments when I was being honest with myself, how it hadn't been so wonderful. I remembered doing things for him that I really didn't like doing, or all the times I had made excuses for him, secretly resenting the fact that he couldn't just compromise for once; all those times I had sacrificed something that I wanted to do in favor of whatever would make *him* happy.

As much as I hated to admit it, as much as I didn't want to feel it, I could see how I had played a part in this disaster, albeit in a very different way: by allowing myself to essentially become invisible and ignoring my own needs and desires. There were multiple aspects to it and my feelings were complicated. Part of me was convinced that if I had done more, been more, he wouldn't have felt the need to go after these other girls. But, at the same time, I was realizing that I had not been honest with him—or myself—in the relationship. When we were together, I had done the best I could, giving him all I knew how to give. And, now? Well, now, I knew better. I had a choice: I could choose to take him back and keep living the same way, or I could stop, and pivot and figure out a new path. Stopping and pivoting felt embarrassing. I didn't want to admit that I had made a mistake in being with Jason, in loving him. But could I really move forward with Jason after this? *Or could I be strong enough and brave enough to choose something different?*

"I'm scared," I told my mom and Grams. "I don't know how all of this works. I don't even know where to start, or if it's even what I want. I know I can't trust him, but I loved him. I don't know what to do." Tears fell into my half-eaten meal as my Grams and mom reached out to me.

"We know, baby, it's hard. We will help you figure this out and face it." I looked into the eyes of those two women and saw such strength there. "We can do this. You can do this," my mom whispered as my Gram nodded in agreement.

We.

Sitting there, wrapped in the arms of these women who had known their own struggles and challenges, I believed them. While I had been crying alone in ~~our~~ my bedroom every night, wondering what I was going to do, they had been talking, coming up with a plan.

I was not alone.

Yet, even with their help, I was completely overwhelmed. I guess this is why some people choose to stay together; getting divorced is fucking *hard*. Where do you start? How much does it cost? What do you do first? Do you have to go to court? I had so many questions, and it was scary to think about starting down that road, not knowing exactly where it would lead.

Over the years, I had developed a whole skill set that had allowed me to be in control of my life—or at least *feel* in control. As a child, I had intuited the best ways to get my father's positive attention and try to avoid his unwanted advances. I had figured out that being a good student and decent at sports made everyone like me and made my father proud of me. The more awards I won and the better behaved I was, the easier things were at home and the more my father seemed to care. An added benefit was that others saw me as being strong, proactive, reliable, efficient, and organized. "Becca's a natural leader!" my teachers said. "She's an amazing girl. We love having her in class." And I loved all of the praise, but in a way, it made me feel even more inadequate and insecure because I knew the only reason I was any of those things was because I was trying so hard to make my father happy and not do anything that would draw more of his negative attention. I had felt like things were going well enough and that I was juggling all the expectations and managing everyone's perception of me, until my mom's suicide attempt. At that point, trying to control things no longer felt like a tool I was using, but more like the only way I knew to survive. Even my own attempt at suicide was an effort to reclaim control when everything else seemed so uncertain.

When I started working and making plans to leave my father's house, I had a new sense of purpose and clarity. Meeting Jason felt like the perfect next step, the best kind of beginning to a new phase of life—being with someone who loved me, getting away from my father, becoming an adult, having control and making my own decisions.

Now, on the other side of this infidelity bomb, I was right back in that place where I had never wanted to be again: having no control over anything.

In moments like this, I couldn't help but think that it was all my fault. I had been so proud of the life I'd built for myself. I'd tied my value to what I had created: this great job, our relationship, our marriage, our house. I'd done my best to hold it all together and here it was, spectacularly shot to hell. The worst part? I hadn't even seen it coming. How shitty and stupid was I?

My mom saw the distress on my face and told me to breathe, probably not even realizing the extent of my anguish. She had been through her own divorce, and I knew I could lean on her. "First, we're going to get you a lawyer, okay?" she said. Her no-nonsense tone helped calm me.

A lawyer. God, that sounded legit. This was real.

"Okay," I whispered.

DEFIANT HOPE

We found a young attorney who seemed like a great fit for me. She had compassion for what I was going through and was very approachable, but she also had a bit of fire in her that made me believe she would fight for me if Jason tried to bullshit his way through this. My lawyer didn't think Jason was going to protest much since he had far more serious criminal charges to deal with. She felt fairly optimistic that the divorce could be finalized within sixty days once the paperwork was filed.

Sixty days? On one hand, it seemed like it might as well be a hundred years, but on the other hand, all of this could be over in two months. I agreed to start the process right then and there, and we served Jason's lawyer with papers the next week.

It was now March, and Jason had been gone for a month. I still had to finish out the school year, seeing and talking to Stephanie about the usual school stuff. My lawyer had instructed me not to talk to her about Jason or her daughter. I felt like such an idiot. Every time I saw her, I remembered confronting her in her classroom, believing myself to be the loyal, righteous wife defending my innocent husband. Now I couldn't even look her in the eye.

I guess she told the principal and assistant principal what was going on, because I was called into the principal's office one day. "I'm sure you know this," she said, "but it's not appropriate for you to talk about what's going on with Stephanie while you're here at school. We don't need any of the other teachers or students to find out about this."

I thought I had been flying under the radar but now I vaguely recalled bad-mouthing Stephanie to a colleague a while ago. Shit. "I understand this must be really hard on you," the principal continued, "but I hope you can keep your focus on the students and your job and not let this affect your work." She was asking the impossible. Of course, I wasn't going to say anything, but I didn't know how I was going to pretend like everything was normal. I would have to figure out how to fake it. I couldn't afford to lose my reputation or possibly—though, unlikely—my job, even though it really sucked having to show up here every day. "As you know, teacher contracts are being renewed next month," she added. "Have you given any thought to what you want to do?"

God dammit. Couldn't I just go one day without having to make yet *another* major decision about my life?

I closed my eyes, wondering if I could speak the truth without falling apart. I felt so incredibly fragile. "Yeah, I don't know, but it's been . . . really, really hard to be here with her. And probably hard for her too. I don't know if I can keep doing this." Thankfully, I managed to get through the conversation without crying.

"Okay, I understand," the principal said. She glanced at the assistant principal then back to me. "If you'd like, we can start looking around at other schools in the district for you to see if they have any positions available." I nodded weakly as she continued, "We'll let you know what we find. You're a good teacher, Becca." With that, I understood that I was dismissed and walked slowly out of the office, not knowing how to feel.

My father had stolen so much from me when I was younger. He'd stolen my carefree mom, my childhood, my autonomy over my body, my willingness to laugh and sing and dance without worrying who might be watching, my desire to be big and bold and bright, my peace, my ability to trust myself. And now it seemed like Jason had taken everything else: my virginity, my heart, my sense of self-worth and self-respect, my school relationships, and now my job on a campus I had loved.

This was such *bullshit*!

————

Along with finding me a lawyer, my mom also found me a support group. Aside from my mom and Grams, I hadn't been speaking to anyone. After Jason was arrested, I took a week off from work and then resolved to spend every non-teaching minute hidden away. For legal reasons, I wasn't supposed to talk to anyone about the ongoing investigation, and for personal reasons, I didn't really want to talk to anyone at all.

My life felt like a humongous lie. All of my coworkers and friends had believed that I was a happy person who led a good life. If more people heard about what had happened, the truth of what my life was *really* like would come out. What they believed was—*had been*—my truth. Yet what I had believed was the truth about my life had been utterly destroyed by the *real* truth, and I wasn't sure I could handle anyone else knowing about that just yet.

After my conversation with the principal, I stayed in my classroom as much as possible. Despite the fact that I was surrounded by students and teachers, I had never felt so alone in my life. I ate my lunch in silence, tucked behind my desk in the darkest, farthest corner of my classroom so no one would know I was in there, and waited for the day to end. I wasn't being the great teacher I wanted to be. I couldn't be that person. She didn't exist anymore. All that was left was a humiliated, betrayed, worthless, angry, and unbelievably sad woman.

I didn't really want to go to the support group because I didn't see how anything could possibly help me. But my mom said it would and, for once, it felt like someone else was making the decisions, which was a relief. As most support groups do, we met in a church auxiliary building and there were light snacks and coffee. My mom came to the first meeting with me, and she shared some of my story so I didn't have to.

For the first two weeks, I didn't say much, but I listened to others tell their stories. Many of their feelings were similar to my own, but their experiences felt more real, more grounded, than mine. My story was so much more embarrassing than theirs. Sure, they felt like their lives and marriages were falling apart, too, but none quite as spectacularly as mine. At least they didn't have the added complications of a spouse's criminal charges to deal with.

During each meeting, the facilitator asked the attendees to share their biggest challenge and greatest victory for the week. At my third meeting, a woman who had been struggling with her self-confidence shared a suggestion someone had given her and how it was helping her through her days. She had been encouraged to write "love notes" to herself. These were notes or letters to remind herself of how great she was, listing out all the amazing qualities about herself that were often overshadowed by negative self-talk. As soon as she began talking about this idea, something inside of me lit up. I barely heard anything else that night.

It was late when the meeting ended, but as soon as I got into my car I grabbed a pen and the only notepad I had with me—a long, skinny one, with a cute elephant at the top and vines winding down the sides. I had originally bought it for making lists, but those narrow papers were now being commandeered for a greater purpose.

The attacks came fast and furious as soon as I began to write. *You're so stupid. This is so stupid*, I thought, as I lifted my pen. Then I wrote, *You are smart and kind*.

You aren't good enough, I thought. I wrote, You are enough.

You're ugly, I thought. I wrote, You are beautiful and sexy.

You're worthless. I am worthy of love and affection.

You should have known he was cheating. I am not responsible for his actions.

I wrote down the opposite of all the negative, destructive thoughts, and then started to list whatever else came to me.

Your eyes sparkle.

You see the best in others.

You're capable of amazing things.

You are loved.

You have family and friends who love and support you.

You didn't do anything wrong.

It's not your fault.

You are fun.

Your smile lights up a room.

I filled page after page after page before I even left the parking lot. I scribbled down positive words about every physical trait, then moved onto affirmations about my personality, skills, and anything else I could think of. On the way home, I kept adding notes, scribbling them down as I waited at stoplights.

I rushed into the house with more than thirty slips of paper, thirty love notes, in my hands. I began taping them on surfaces around the house where I would see them most often: the bathroom mirrors, my nightstand, the refrigerator, the back of the front door. I taped the notes inside of kitchen cabinets, hall closets, dresser drawers, on the sides of the TV. I tucked them into my bed sheets, my books, the glove box in my car, my jewelry box, and even my winter boots.

I didn't care if it looked ridiculous. With each skinny flag I posted, I was reclaiming lost territory.

Satisfied with my work, I started getting ready for bed. I felt a spark of joy just seeing all my notes scattered around the room.

———

Emboldened by my elephant notes, I decided to go for a brisk walk the next morning with Bianca loping along at my side. Man, it felt good to sweat. My face was red with exertion and my arms and legs were pumping. I was struggling, but it felt good to move my body.

I rounded the corner of my street and slowed to a walk, cooling down as I approached my house. I unlocked the front door and let Bianca go straight for her water bowl. When I walked past the TV, one of my notes caught my eye: *What your father did was not okay. You are a survivor.*

Immediately, I felt a division slice through my body, like someone had cut me in half.

Is that note really true?

The question popped into my mind before I could stop it. *Of course it's true!* a fierce voice inside of me insisted. But another, more familiar voice, answered calmly, gently challenging: *how do you know?*

Well, that there was the real question. How *did* I know if that sentiment was true or not? Last night, in a moment of confidence and inspiration, I had jotted down all these nice things about myself and reminders of my personal beliefs. But writing them down didn't necessarily make them *true*. How could I honestly say that what I had written was any more or less true than what I'd believed before? What made *anything* "true"?

My main conviction was that the things I'd been believing before had led me *here*. Into a life where I had practically disappeared as I became whatever others wanted me to be. A life where I hadn't been able to accept that my husband was cheating on me, even when people I trusted told me to my face. That wasn't a life I wanted to live anymore.

Creating new truths for myself, or at least introducing new ideas of what *could* be true, seemed like my only option if I wanted things to be different. I had to decide what was "true" for me, and I had to choose to believe it.

The word "truth" is so loaded. People talk about truth as if it's a black and white thing, but there are a million shades of gray. As a kid, I'd grown up memorizing Bible verses in church and hearing about "God's truth." Then I had my father filling my mind with his ideas of what was good and okay. *"You're just taking a shower, Becca. You don't need to be embarrassed. This is totally normal."* I thought back to that girl who didn't know what the fuck to believe, who was trying to make sense of what her body was saying and what her father was saying, and which one was "right" when they gave her conflicting messages. I didn't understand back then that I could have beliefs implanted in my mind, have this voice feeding me ideas, but that voice wasn't necessarily *mine*. And when Jason came along, I didn't realize that those other voices were still in there, keeping me confused and afraid.

Over the last few months, though, as I had wrestled with what and who to believe, I had begun to sense that there wasn't necessarily a golden standard of absolute truth for all things, all people, but rather there was *my truth*. My truth was determined by me and what I chose to believe about myself. Yet it was even deeper than that. It was a knowing within me. An instant internal recognition that left me almost vibrating, sizzling. I didn't need anyone else to teach me what was true for me or not, I could *feel it*. My truth came from within. And this place was where the words on those love notes had come from. They hadn't originated from this surface-Becca, or what someone else had said to me. Those words had been birthed from that quiet defiance. They had gushed forth from this deep well of knowledge within me, not from my head but my heart, my soul. They had tumbled recklessly over each other onto the page, my truths desperate to be spoken and heard.

No, I didn't think just changing a few words turned something into an absolute truth, but I did know that the words I spoke to myself could be powerful.

I read the note in front of me again, sensing into my body for that gut reaction, to know if I could trust myself and believe what I had written. I knew that place inside of me existed, but it could still be really, really hard to find. At that moment, I couldn't find it.

Okay, I thought, *let's try something else.* I read the words out loud, putting a different spin on them. "What your father did was totally okay. You are not a survivor of anything." Wham.

My body responded immediately that time, instantly stiffening up like a wall, everything in me rebelled against that "truth." Well, at least now I had some clarity.

This was going to be a long, slow process. I couldn't expect my brain or body to rewire itself overnight. Years of negative self-talk had worn deep ruts into my mind. I was trying to pull myself out of those pits of despair and find my way back to who I really was.

WILL THE TRUE ME PLEASE STAND UP?

"**I** know it's been a while and I should be over it by now, but I'm still just heartbroken," the woman sobbed as we sat in our support group one evening. "I don't know what to do with my life anymore!" Others around the circle nodded sympathetically, and I reached over to hand the woman a tissue. I appreciated this space but as I continued to attend this group each week, I was beginning to grow bored of all the sorrow. I felt for these people, for myself, but it was all just starting to sound like so much suffering and sadness. Where did it end? *When* did it end? Some of these people had been in the separation or divorce process for years.

Each time I left the group, I found myself thinking about the people I'd met there and how it didn't seem like their stories changed much from week to week. It was always the same, like there was this pattern of grief that we couldn't escape. Writing the love notes to myself had stirred something new within me, and that feeling was like the crest of a wave I wanted to keep riding—maybe *had* to keep riding, to lift me up and over this cycle of powerlessness and self-pity.

I didn't blame anyone for feeling however they felt, and their experiences were so different from mine, there was almost no comparison anyway. But I was noticing that my own feelings of hopelessness and grief were shifting. The initial shock and sadness seemed to be wearing off. Instead of feeling sorry for myself and those in my group, I started getting mad.

There was a growing rage for all the shit that had been thrown at us, that we were left to sort through. And I began to feel those sparks of anger kindling brighter within me. Not surprisingly, my anger was focused primarily on Jason. More than anything, I still wanted to know *why*. *Why* had he done this to me?

One evening, I couldn't take it any longer. I had to know. I had to get my answers. I paced the bedroom and dialed Jason's cell phone. Hearing him say hello was the only green light I needed for my barrage of questions. As I shot off my *whys* like a series of cannons, volatile and destructive and explosive, I escalated to a yell and was half-crying, half-screaming my need to know.

"Why did you do this to me, you asshole?! Why did you sleep with her? Why did you cheat on me? What were you thinking? Did you ever even love me? Why did you lie to me? Why did you do this?! Tell me! TELL ME!"

Suddenly, the voice of Jason's dad broke through. "Becca! Becca! This isn't helping anyone. You need to stop."

As I tried to calm down, he proceeded to tell me how sad and sorry Jason was and that he still wanted to be with me. He said that he and Jason's mom had been through hard times and they had worked things out, so they knew we could get through this.

"Becca, why don't you come to Brownsville and stay here for a while? You and Jason can talk and we can help you work this out."

Holy shit. He did not just say that. Did I hear that right? Come to Brownsville and forgive Jason? Okay, yeah, sure. I'll get right on that.

What the fuck?

I laughed out loud and said, "That's BULLSHIT! We are not getting back together and I'm not coming to Brownsville!" I hung up, fuming. I was done. Really done. I was done being sad about him, about the relationship we'd had, the way it had ended, and the way it could have been.

It was time for him to go.

I still had some boxes left over from when we moved into the house, so I pulled those out of the storage closet and began packing his remaining things. Or maybe it was more like picking up trash and chucking it into the garbage. However you want to say it, the point is, I got rid of all his crap and banished the boxes to the garage alongside the infidelity couches.

———

The next week, I was ready to share at the support group. I was still seriously pissed off in the wake of the conversation with Jason and his dad. All the time. Rage coursed through me, constantly burning in my chest. I managed to rein it in while I was at work so I could maintain some semblance of professionalism, but at home, I seethed with anger.

My feelings were becoming so intense and more and more difficult to contain. I wasn't used to letting others in, but at this point, the support group was the closest thing I had to friends. I had become more and more isolated—and, I now understood, silenced—during the years I'd made Jason my main priority. I had become a shell of myself. I didn't feel like I knew who I was anymore without him. My wants, needs, desires, goals, dreams, and thoughts were all for him. The strangers at the support group were kind, but I hadn't yet shared my whole story, so I didn't feel fully invested. No one knew me. At least, not the *real* me. There was so much inside of me that I wasn't saying. I needed an outlet, a safe place to vent, and the support group made the most sense.

At the meeting, I sat there, head down, quiet as usual, listening to the others share. When the last person finished speaking, I closed my eyes and slowly raised my hand. Still unable to look around the room, I spoke softly, staring at my feet. "I'm Becca. I'm twenty-four years old and I filed for divorce from my husband two months ago. I thought he was a really great guy, you know? Like, I really believed that he loved me and we were happy and we had a pretty good life." My voice began to grow stronger as I continued. "I met him when I was nineteen . . . " As the words flowed out of me, I spoke louder and louder, my voice filling the space, fueled by my rage and this sudden desire to no longer be silent. It was about damn time I got this stuff off my chest. I raised my head and met their eyes. "And then I found out that he had been sleeping with my coworker's daughter the whole time we've been married."

Everyone was listening to me, murmuring their support and empathy as I told my story. With each word, the grip that had been tightening around me for weeks, crushing me under its weight, slowly began to loosen. I had become so used to this feeling of being suffocated that I just assumed it was going to be my new normal: I would spend the rest of my life struggling to breathe, forcing myself to speak. But now, *now*, I could feel my lungs expanding a little more. Like verbalizing the truth somehow cleared out my internal, emotional space in the same way that packing Jason's things had cleared out my external, physical space.

As I was sharing, it hit me that I didn't care if these people liked me or not. I wasn't sharing *for them*, or to earn their love or affection, or to get their attention. No, I was doing this *for me*. I had been scared to drop my mask and speak out with brutal honesty, to tell others what was going on inside of me. This was an entirely new experience and one that I had always tried to avoid.

But giving voice to everything I'd been going through felt validating and real. Being in the support group had shown me that people go through shit *all the time*. Yet I felt like I had to hide my own story, my own pain, and I felt totally alone. I was physically, mentally, and emotionally exhausted, not just because of the pain of all of this, but because I felt I had to fake my happiness through it. I didn't want to accept that this was happening to me, so I put on a persona, trying to tell the world with my face, my voice, my body language that I was fine, strong, totally able to handle this. I felt like I had to present an entirely different person to the world, a person who was not experiencing what I was experiencing, because that felt safe to me and less vulnerable. But it was fucking exhausting.

That night at the support group, I realized that it was okay to feel what I was feeling; okay to be in the situation that I was going through. By opening myself up, I took a risk, but it also felt like releasing a pressure valve. I could finally begin taking off my mask and armor and just be *me*.

Everyone likes the end of the journey, the final result, but no one likes going through all the crap you have to go through to get there. As I heard the words coming out of my mouth, it felt like I was outside of my body, thinking, *There I am, this is me getting through this.* It felt so powerful to just be real and not worry about what anyone else thought of me or my story. Maybe I looked weak, or ridiculous, or pitiful, or stupid, but so what? I didn't have to be ashamed. No one there had everything figured out. No one anywhere has the perfect life. And no one could understand exactly what it was like to be me, just like I couldn't understand exactly what it was like to be them. We may not get each other's shit but that's okay. We were all in this together, and it felt so freeing to admit that life could be pretty fucked up sometimes.

I looked around at these people who were listening, really listening to me, and I felt so grateful that they had taken off their masks too. They had let down their guard, dropped their walls, and it gave me the courage and the safety to be real too.

I was still angry and I still had complicated divorce shit to deal with; I was still sad and I still had to grieve the loss of my marriage and what I had imagined my future to be. Sharing my story didn't solve anything. But that single act of sharing was an act of defiance. It was me jumping out of my father's car again, the warrior who refused to stay silent. I had realized that by not sharing, by not ever telling anyone what was really happening with me, I was literally silencing myself. I didn't want anyone else dictating what I could and couldn't do, what I could and couldn't say. Sharing with the group felt like a big *fuck you* to silence, and it felt GOOD. I felt powerful. Strong. I was a thousand pounds lighter. By sharing my story in a matter-of-fact way, I had taken it *out of me* and allowed it to become real. With the truth out in the open, another new feeling was emerging; one that I couldn't exactly name, but that felt a lot like acceptance.

As I drove home from group that night, I reflected on all the ways I had been perpetuating an environment of silence. Not just the silence of my actual voice, but of *me*; who I was, what I liked and disliked, how I wanted to spend my time and live my life. Considering this, I asked myself what I was missing out on, and how could I change that? How could I reengage with myself and the world again? Could I choose to live differently?

I started to remember things that I enjoyed, things that used to make me happy. For instance, I had really enjoyed playing sports in high school. When things were so hard with my mom and my father, sports had been the bright spot in my week. I suddenly missed the physical workouts, the camaraderie, and the friendship. I could have that again, right? I just had to figure out how adults played sports and made friends. It felt like a mystery and more than a little overwhelming to think about reinventing my life. But I told myself to keep it simple.

I thought about my volleyball experience. I remembered the circuit workouts that we did in the off-season. Just a set of different exercises, repeated a couple of times. I didn't need to go to a gym or buy any equipment. As a plan started to form in my mind, I felt intoxicated by the possibilities.

I did my first workout after school the next day. I had not exercised since high school. Jason never exercised, and I had spent the last five years working on getting my degree and spending time with him. My circuit was very basic: different variations of squats, some lunges, as many push-ups as I could manage, and crunches. I turned up the music and repeated all the moves three times. By the end, I was out of breath and sweating. I felt fucking fantastic! I also noticed that my anger seemed to loosen up a little more, as if it had been jarred free with movement. My cheeks actually hurt from smiling. *I* was in charge of myself, and I could choose to be strong. I could choose to move my body and I could choose to do things that made me happy.

From that point on, I did my circuits when I got home from work every day. I varied the exercises as I got stronger and more curious about what else I could do. Not too long after starting my new routine, I began taking long walks with Bianca in the evenings. Along the way, I reconnected with a friend from high school who had moved into my neighborhood. We walked together every once in a while and occasionally went out to dinner. I had forgotten what it was like to have a friend, and just those brief chats seemed to open up something else inside of me.

My new focus on exercise made me reconsider my diet too. Jason and I had spent most of our time together eating out, and although I had been surrounded by food while working as a server, I had not picked up any cooking skills. So I started experimenting with recipes and trying out techniques I had seen on the Food Network. Having the TV on helped fill the silence in my empty house, and the shows also provided inspiration as I tried to figure out what I liked to do. Whether it was a chef suggesting a new meal or a sitcom character out riding a bike, I found myself intrigued by other people's hobbies. *Hmmm*, I would think. *Maybe I could try that.* So I did.

My love notes were still plastered all over the house. I stood in front of them and read them out loud to myself so that I could actually hear the words spoken out into the world. I felt weird telling myself how pretty or kind I was before I left my house for the day, but it made a difference to speak the words into the silence. It didn't take long before I had most of them memorized, and the phrases came to mind at random moments throughout the day. Any time my negative self-talk started back up, I could recognize those old thoughts as false and replace them with my new truths from my notes.

Each day that passed after Jason's arrest felt like a tiny victory in and of itself. All these new things I was doing were expanding my vision wider and wider. I no longer felt like I was drowning under an ocean of grief and anger. I could finally begin to catch glimpses of a way forward, to see what life could be like without him.

Although I was still attending the support group, I missed being around other people I could talk to. I missed having a team, whether it was being on a sports team or working at the restaurant with other servers. I wanted friends. I wanted connection, but I didn't know how to get it. I thought back to past times when I had felt deeply connected with someone. The first person who came to mind was my old boyfriend, the guy I dated in high school before I met Jason. We had a lot of history together, and maybe it was possible that he still cared about me. Maybe we could just pick up where we'd left off. I didn't stop long enough to consider how much time had passed since we'd last been in touch, and that a lot could have happened between now and then.

I was thrilled when he responded to my text. After one phone call, he invited me out to dinner. I felt relieved. This was a no-brainer, an easy fix to my loneliness. I didn't exactly think of him as a replacement, but here was someone who used to care about me, maybe even love me, and perhaps we could feel that way again. *Easy* sounded so wonderful in that moment.

Though dinner was a little uncomfortable, it went well. Well enough that we decided to go find something else fun to do after dinner. As we considered our options, we began reminiscing about the past.

We started laughing, remembering some old inside jokes, and then he quieted and looked at me curiously. "Wait, didn't you break up with me?" he asked, in a nonchalant way—as if he didn't remember exactly what happened, when I knew that he did.

I nodded sheepishly.

"God, that was an awful time. You really broke my heart." For a moment, he seemed to be reliving that hurt and was now trying to determine where we should go from here. But with those memories lingering between us, the damage was done. He tried to shrug it off, but the imaginary bubble of ease and happiness I'd been floating in broke and reality came rushing back.

He offered one more suggestion for where we could go, but I interrupted him. "Never mind, you can just take me home." The car was quiet as he drove toward my house. Yes, I had broken up with him. How could I have forgotten that? I felt embarrassed and ashamed that I had simply used him just for the possibility of falling into someone else's loving arms. "I'm sorry," I said, turning to look at him one last time before exiting the car. He gave a little smile, nodded, and then drove away after I reached my front door.

My little elephant notes fluttered as I walked down the hallway and tossed my purse on the bed. In the bathroom, I saw the love notes on my mirror and read them again. *You are beautiful. You are enough.* The notes felt like anchors, grounding me.

That evening made it clear that I needed to move forward with who I was *now*, rather than trying to go back to some previous version of myself. I didn't want to just re-create or build upon the past. It actually felt like I had a clean slate, a blank page. This was a new chapter in my life and, to honor that, I had to keep trying new things, not fall back on what would be easy. I had to fully trust myself with my future.

REIGNITING THE SPARK WITHIN

There really should be a class on how to meet people and make friends as an adult. Although that night with my ex-boyfriend had ended poorly, laughing and talking with him, and spending time with my one other friend, had made me realize just how much I had missed hanging out with people. I was craving companionship and friendship after having pretty much isolated myself up to this point in my adult life. Trying to figure out where to begin finding people my own age felt like a mystery, especially when the easy option of "work friends" had been completely taken off the table.

I had heard other teachers at school talk about Myspace and Facebook, these new websites where you could connect with people over music and shared interests, or find old high school or college friends. The websites seemed like a good place to start—they were free and all I had to do was set up an account. Easy enough.

One Saturday morning, I made a profile page on Myspace and began looking for people who lived near-ish. I had always seemed to connect well with both girls and guys, so I was open to meeting anyone. I found about ten people who lived close enough to contact so I sent them a message.

Hi, my name is Becca. I'm wanting to meet new friends in the area. I came across your profile and wanted to get to know you better. You can return this message here. :)

At the time, I thought I sounded friendly and nice. And I was damn proud of myself for being brave and reaching out to strangers. It felt good to be doing *something*, to be proactive and put myself out there in a new way.

I hit *send* and instantly felt a little giddy. I was taking risks! Until this whole disaster with Jason, I had prided myself on being a planner, organized, always anticipating what was going to happen next. My recent efforts to try new things and be more spontaneous felt like learning a new language. It was a little messy, really vulnerable, and kind of scary. In the last month, I had gone to a farmers market for the first time, gone running for fun, tried sushi, tried alcohol (a piña colada wine spritzer), and gone to a movie on a school night. I was flexing my muscles, both literally and figuratively, making decisions for myself.

What was strange and surprising to me was how often I felt like I had to give myself permission to try something. This usually meant having an internal conversation with myself that, honestly, made me feel a little crazy at times. First, I reminded myself that *I mattered*—I could do something for myself that sounded fun, even if someone else might think it was stupid or silly or childish. I reminded myself that my interests and desires were valid. I also reminded myself that there was no pressure for me to do *anything*! When I noticed those voices in my head having mental debates about a decision, I took a deep breath and acknowledged that I didn't have to make a choice right then; I could just say *maybe* and keep thinking about it, or come back to it later.

In all of this, I wasn't exactly sure who I was arguing with. Maybe some version of my old self? All I knew is that there were all these other voices fighting against the new *me* that was emerging, trying to pull me back down. I knew the old ruts of insecurity and doubt were deep, so I kept laying new thoughts beside them, hoping these paths I was creating would soon become more well-worn and easily traveled.

So here I was now, doing my best to heal all these unhealthy wounds of feeling unloved and abandoned and unworthy that had been infecting me for years. I was discovering that, while I had been shoving all that shit deep inside myself, sewing it up tight so no one else would know it was there, I had suffocated the real me. I thought a lot about the little girl I'd been who danced in circles in her princess costumes, singing her heart out and delighting in life, who was awed by the miraculous hot dog maker and splashed happily in the tub with her sister and mom. I had to believe that my full self-expression was still inside of me somewhere. She had been covered up by pain and trauma and coping mechanisms and there was no quick fix to save her. Little by little, I was cutting away old sutures and scraping away the decay. I was removing all the shit that had settled into the tight corners of my heart and mind, and applying the healing balms of self-care, curiosity, patience, and gentleness with myself.

Time does not, itself, heal us. We heal ourselves by investing the time it takes to do so. I had made a choice to begin that healing process, even though circumstances beyond my control had forced me to get to that point. Now, I was committed to finding that spunky girl within me again. That quiet defiance that had shown itself here and there was urging me on, embodying both the one who was searching and the one waiting to be found.

Like a child learning to walk, I was practicing trusting myself. With each hesitant step, I grew more confident, and more of that outgoing, sparkly little girl began to shine through the muck. Jason's betrayal had left me feeling more alone than I ever had in my life, but being alone meant that I had to learn how to rely on myself for almost everything, especially for love.

I wasn't half-assing my healing or shoving those big emotions deep inside and ignoring them. I was allowing myself to feel all of those dark, heavy feelings, and loving myself through them. I might feel really sad and cry my eyeballs out, but then I'd notice, *Oh, look at that! I feel better now.* I was figuring out what brought me comfort. I was noticing how my thoughts about myself were changing, and how the love notes were rewiring my self-talk. It was a one-step-forward, two-steps-back sort of thing for a while. But now, instead of trying to be who someone else wanted me to be, I was growing more comfortable letting the real me speak up.

I understood that some aspects of my divorce made it easier for me to process all of my emotions so quickly. I had noticed that I was moving through the stages of grief a lot faster than some other people in my support group. For one, Jason and I didn't have kids. Our separation hadn't really affected anyone except for the two of us. In that way, our divorce was actually pretty simple. Although I thought I had wanted a baby with him, I could appreciate how having children would have made the experience far more complicated and difficult than it already was. Also, there was a finality to my situation that the others didn't have: Jason was dealing with criminal charges with consequences that could involve him going to prison. Although that fact was hard for me to accept initially, it did mean that I was able to just cut and run. I didn't have to interact with Jason or see him ever again if I didn't want to. Because of these circumstances, I was having a very different experience than the rest of those in my group. Although I was still attending the weekly sessions, I felt ready to put the anger and sadness behind me (for the most part) and start exploring what was on the other side.

———

After I'd sent my Myspace message, I left for the grocery store with a bit of sass in my step. Reaching out to strangers online felt risky, but also really exciting. This was another huge leap outside of my comfort zone. When I returned home that afternoon, I was delighted to see that I had a response. The message was from a guy named Darren who lived in the next town over. His profile showed that he was still online, so I immediately messaged him back. Thus began a marathon of messaging each other on Myspace, then exchanging phone numbers and texting, then finally talking on the phone. All on the same day, in an eight-hour span.

Darren was cool and fun and seemed easygoing and confident. We had been enjoying our conversation and decided to meet in person at Taco Cabana. As I drove the twenty minutes to meet him, I felt so proud of myself. I had made another friend!

Darren and I hung out at Taco Cabana for an hour before walking around the shopping center, eventually relaxing into rocking chairs outside one of the department stores. We chatted away until 3:00 a.m. Our conversation moved effortlessly from surface-level topics to deeper, more meaningful ones. Finally, we were both exhausted, so we gave each other a quick hug and headed home.

Later that morning, I thought about all the things I *hadn't* told Darren. Not that it was a big deal, we had only known each other a few hours. But, to be honest, there had been a mutual attraction and I didn't know what to do about that. I was still working on myself and had sworn off romance after that disastrous rebound attempt with my ex-boyfriend. Besides, I was technically still married to Jason since our divorce hadn't yet been finalized. I didn't want to lead Darren on, but I also couldn't make myself cut off this first real opportunity for friendship.

The way I saw it, I had three options. One, I could stop this friendship before even starting. I wouldn't have to tell him anything. I didn't have to contact him again, and I could let things end with little consequence. Two, I could continue hanging out with him and pretend that my life hadn't just exploded. Three, I could tell him the truth about who I was and what I was experiencing and see what happened.

The first option made me feel sad and disappointed. The second option sounded too much like my old habits and made me cringe. That option also was too much like lying and—well, I'd had enough lies to last me a lifetime. But the third option . . . that one represented the true me. Those few times over the last couple of months when I had been honest and upfront about my situation and myself had given me the greatest sense of freedom I'd felt in a decade or more. My body had become so familiar with shutting down and closing off that the drastic shift to being more open felt like letting a horse out of the gate—the internal response to sharing my truth was jolting and instantaneous and exciting.

Of course, if I told Darren the truth, it was entirely possible that he might want nothing to do with me. But, in my mind, I would have at least shown up, *fully*, as a whole person. I wanted to be myself, scars and all.

The following night, we went to Chili's for dinner. The hostess sat us in a small two-person booth. I knew that I wanted to let him in. I wanted to be honest with him. But aside from sharing with my mom and at my support group, no one else knew the full truth. I did not want to start a new . . . whatever this was . . . with Darren by putting on a mask and pretending like things were okay. I did not want to put on my usual set of armor and act like I wasn't in pain. This would be the real me, showing up, sharing all my shit, and not hiding out of fear that I would be found lacking.

Halfway through our meal, I laid all of my cards on the table.

"So," I started, "I have some things I wanted to tell you about. There's . . . " I paused and took a drink, trying to calm my nerves. "There's a lot of craziness in my life right now, and I feel like it's only right if I'm honest with you about it."

I told him about Jason, and how he cheated on me, the charges that had been filed against him. I talked about Stephanie and how it felt to see her at work every day. I described how I was feeling and explained how I was working on myself. I told him about exercising and writing my love notes and going to the support group. My hands were shaking as I fiddled with my napkin, folding and refolding it a hundred times. I wasn't ready to tell him—or anyone yet—about everything with my father and my past. But all that seemed almost irrelevant compared to what had happened with Jason. I no longer believed that I was totally damaged or that I was completely worthless, but I didn't know how others would see me and if they would think the same.

"I feel like a new person in a lot of ways. I really don't know if I'm even ready for a friendship, although I really want to connect with people. I just need to figure shit out. It's a lot, I know. And if this is all too much for you, I understand. I just felt like you deserve to know and also that I needed to be true to myself."

I grabbed my drink and sat back in the booth, holding the straw in my mouth so that I would stop talking. The silence was excruciating. I could hardly look at him. But at the same time, I was so fucking proud of myself.

I had no idea what he would say. His response was out of my control. Strangely, I was okay with that. I sat across from him at the table, feeling the uncertainty of the moment deep in my belly. I had a new confidence that, no matter what he said or did, I would be fine—I had made it through far worse—but I hoped he wouldn't walk away.

I put my drink down and leaned forward again. I ventured to raise my eyes and found that Darren was leaning forward as well.

His face was totally relaxed, except for a slight smile. "I'm in," he said.

———

A month or so later, Darren and I were hanging out. I had continued to be very open about what was happening with the divorce and how naive I felt about not knowing that Jason was cheating on me. "God, when I think about it, it just makes me feel so dumb," I said.

"You're not dumb," Darren reassured me. Then, tilting his head and furrowing his brow, he added, "I bet you're smarter than you think you are, actually. Just because people treat you poorly, make you feel stupid, or mistreat your trust doesn't mean they're right. I mean, have you ever taken an IQ test?"

"What?" I asked. "Are you serious?" Even with all the time we'd been spending together, I still couldn't always tell when he was joking.

"Yes, I'm serious," he said. "Why don't you take one? Then you'll know the truth." He went over to my computer and started searching for an online test.

Of course I knew that, to some degree, I was smart. I had done well in high school and college—in fact, I prided myself on being an excellent student—and I was a teacher. Clearly, some cylinders were firing. I could trust my abilities when it came to taking classes and passing exams, because there, the expectations were clear. I could memorize facts and read the books and regurgitate the material. But when it came to more abstract things like relationships and, well, *life*, I'd been told by my father for so long that I just didn't understand how it all worked, and then I'd been completely humiliated and caught off guard by Jason's infidelity, and the only explanation I could come up with was that I was stupid.

In the end, the number I got on the IQ test didn't necessarily matter, although it did surprise me. What did matter was a brand-new realization: I was *intelligent*. Like, objectively, measurably intelligent. I was not stupid. I was not worthless or crazy. Maybe I didn't always know what to do in a situation, but I had my own kind of wisdom and knowledge inside of me. As I stared at the number on the screen, the words I had written on my elephant notes embedded themselves a little deeper. *I am smart. I am capable. I can trust myself.*

My friendship with Darren was challenging me in many new ways. He didn't let me get away with anything simply because

I'd had a difficult past. He asked hard questions and when I made excuses or avoided topics, he constantly asked me *why?* or *why not?* Before, I would have been annoyed or offended or afraid of his prodding, but now, being asked to explore my beliefs and confront old habits felt encouraging and welcome. Most of the time.

"Becca, you don't need to keep saying sorry," he said one night, after I kept apologizing about burning our dinner.

"Sorry, I just—" I replied, catching myself and sighing loudly. "I know! I don't know why I do it. It's like a habit. I don't even realize I'm doing it."

"Well, you don't have to do it with me, *ever*, okay?" He spoke kindly. "I think you're great. Dinner is a bit crispy, yes, but you don't have to be perfect all the time. It's okay to mess up sometimes." The ease with which he said the words and smiled at me was real, and I felt myself relax a little more.

Saying "I'm sorry" had become my tried and true way to dissolve tension, divert anger, or reduce negative reactions from my father. I had used it so often with him that I unconsciously used it with others. Apologizing became a tool I could use—to please people and make sure they liked me, or to control situations or reactions. As Darren brought it to my attention, I began to notice that I said sorry for everything, not just when I did something wrong or hurt someone. I was apologizing for walking, talking, breathing, existing!

Darren was a great example of someone who lived *unapologetically*. Just by virtue of being around him, I became more aware of how often I said sorry, or asked for permission, or tried to make others happy, because it was so obvious that he *didn't* do those things.

One night, we went out for sushi. The restaurant was really nice, and we had made reservations. When we arrived and checked in, the hostess led us to a table where one person had to sit in a booth, and the other in a chair opposite. Darren and I sat down, me on the booth side. After the hostess walked away, Darren calmly stood up and started to turn the table sideways. I was mortified.

"Oh my god! What are you doing?" I hissed. "You can't do that!"

He looked up, laughing. "Why not?"

Having worked in restaurants before, I knew why tables were arranged the way they were.

"They set these up like this for a reason!" I whispered loudly, trying not to cause a scene. "And they might get mad if we move it around! Someone might come over here and make you move it back. We could get in trouble."

"So what?" he shrugged. "It's more comfortable like this." He came around the side and sat down beside me, smiling from ear to ear. "And, now I get to sit next to you."

He may have been more comfortable, but I sat there stiff and uncertain. There was no one else close to us and the restaurant wasn't that busy, but I just knew that someone was going to complain.

"Becca," Darren said, leaning into me, intuiting what I was feeling, "it's okay to ask for what you want, or to just make it happen yourself." I took a deep breath, wanting to believe that he was right, but fighting against my decades of training that asking for what I wanted would be met with rebuke and punishment.

As the server approached our table, my body tensed, ready to jump up, apologize, and reset the table.

"Oh, perfect!" she exclaimed. "I'm glad you adjusted the table. Are you okay here? Or would you prefer to be seated somewhere else?"

Darren looked at me, eyes twinkling, and said, "It's okay, I think we're fine here now."

I was shocked, stupefied. How had that worked? I could not believe it hadn't been a big deal. We hadn't gotten into trouble. The server had actually congratulated us! I turned to Darren, in awe.

What was this new, magical experience of asking for what I wanted, of desiring something and making it happen? Not fearing that I would get in trouble, but having the confidence that regardless of what the consequences were, I would figure it out.

SHE WAS THERE
THE WHOLE TIME

SUMMER 2009

I n the next week following that dinner with Darren, I was checking my banking accounts online when I noticed something odd. There was a withdrawal request for the full balance of my home escrow account. For the past six months, I'd been putting extra money from my checks into escrow to help cover the upcoming property taxes. Having a new home meant property taxes would be higher the second year, so I had been advised to save extra to prepare. Concerned, I called the bank.

"Yes, ma'am," the representative confirmed. "That's correct. There is a withdrawal request for the balance."

Jason.

"Okay. Well, I'd like you to deny that request, please," I said firmly, already furious.

"I'm sorry, ma'am, I can't do that. He's a co-owner; his name is on the account."

Crap. I argued with her for a few more minutes explaining the situation before realizing I wasn't going to get anywhere. *That piece of shit!* I hung up the phone and called my lawyer.

I had been playing so nicely through this whole divorce process to get through it as quickly and easily as possible: I'll take what's mine, you take what's yours. I just wanted him to go away. But now? Now, I was pissed; smoke was practically coming out of my ears.

I called Darren that afternoon as I furiously paced around the house, stumbling upon a box of those pictures from Disney World tucked away in one of the upstairs bedrooms.

I told Darren about Jason trying to withdraw from the escrow account and how angry I was. The divorce wasn't even final yet! Neither of us was supposed to touch the accounts. "I'm staring at these pictures of us and I just want to get rid of them. I just want to fucking *burn* them!" I picked up a handful of photos and smashed them back down into the box.

"Okay," he said. "Why don't you?"

"Wait, what? Seriously? I can do that?" I asked, his question suddenly lighting up a different part of my brain.

"I mean, yeah, if you want to. They're your pictures, right? You can do whatever the hell you want with them. If you want to burn them, we can get a can and start a fire and you can just throw 'em in."

Good thing Darren had some ideas because I had no fucking clue how to safely do something like that. I had wanted to burn the infidelity couches, but a bonfire of that size sounded scary. Plus, according to the current divorce agreement, I was supposed to give the couches back to Jason. But a metal can and some old photos—*my* photos? I could handle that.

Darren showed up with a metal bucket, a lighter, some wood, and a poking stick. I wanted to be in charge of the fire and to put the pictures in myself. Darren stayed back, offering a few basic instructions as I wielded the lighter like a blowtorch. I felt powerful, in control, and in charge. I tossed the first photo in and watched it crumple in on itself. Then I threw in another and another and another. It took some time to burn all of them as I stared, mesmerized by the flickering light. As the fire grew brighter and the images turned to ash, I felt like the phoenix rising. *I* was in those pictures. But those pictures were of a very different person than who I was now. The warrior-Becca I was simultaneously becoming and rediscovering watched as the old me disappeared into the flames.

———

The following week, my attorney called with an update on the escrow account. She had contacted Jason's lawyer about the funds and they had managed to come to a tentative new agreement. "Jason will give you the money back," she said, "but apparently, there's a few things they still want."

"Okay, like what?" I asked.

She explained, "They want the coffee table that was paid for in cash by his mom, and they want his Nintendo Wii."

I raised my eyebrows and scoffed. "So, you're saying that this could all be over if I just give him the fucking table and his video games?"

"Yes."

"Well, shit, take them! I don't care!" I was so ready to be done with him.

"Oh, and there's one more thing," she said. "He also wants some pictures."

"Pictures?" I repeated, trying to hold in a giggle at the audacity and strangeness of the request.

"Yes, from the relationship, from Disney World, other vacations, that sort of thing."

I laughed. "Um, so, those are no longer available."

"Okay . . . " she paused. "Can you be more specific?"

I could still smell the smoke when I walked into the backyard. I turned now and glanced out the window at the metal can on the patio. "I burned them." I took in a breath and held it, waiting to hear what she would say. Would this mess things up?

"Ah. Okay. Alright. Well, I think we can still make this work." I could hear her scribbling down her notes. "Coffee table and Nintendo Wii, but no pictures. Got it!"

I exhaled in a rush, joy and relief flooding through me.

In the end, Jason and his lawyer signed the documents. We still had to exchange items per the agreement, but that seemed trivial. The decree stated that he had to pay me the required funds and *then* he could get his shit out of *my* garage.

———

Jason and his parents were on their way to my house to hand me a check and pick up the rest of his shit. After today, he would really and truly be out of my life for good. I was nervous. I hadn't seen him since I dropped him off at the hotel. I got up from the couch and started walking around the living room, rearranging the things on my new coffee table, straightening the bookshelves, and fluffing the pillows. When I opened the closet door to get the vacuum out, one of my love notes fluttered, nearly tickling my nose.

You are strong. You can do hard things.

The words called me out and dared me to doubt them.

My house was already clean. It was always clean now that Jason was gone. I was anxious about our meeting, trying to distract myself. But, *I was strong.* I could do this. I went back to the couch and sat down. *Breathe, just breathe,* I told myself. I closed my eyes and inhaled deeply, held it for a second, then slowly let it out. Again. One more time. Okay. *Now,* I thought, *notice what I am feeling.* That was harder. I continued to breathe intentionally, part of my awareness on my breath, the other part trying to feel into my body. I had ignored my body for so long that it still took a while for me to tune into what I was physically experiencing. It felt like I was in a new relationship, not with another person, but with myself. *Come on, it's okay, you can talk to me. I'm listening.*

I'm afraid.

I'm sad.

I want to show him that I've changed.

I don't want to be weak.

Another deep breath. *Okay, why am I feeling this way?*

Because he hurt me. Because I don't know how this is gonna go. Because I can't control what he's going to do or say. Because I'm still not sure I can trust myself to not give in to him.

I could feel the tightness in my throat, the clenching of every muscle, like a gazelle poised to flee from an advancing lion. I kept breathing slowly and deeply to reassure my body that I was safe. I rubbed my legs, reassuring them that they could relax. In my mind, I pictured myself sitting next to a beautiful pond, the sunshine warming my face, Bianca frolicking in the grass. "I am safe," I whispered. "You are safe." I gave myself a little hug, feeling my heartbeat slowing and my body beginning to soften. A new thought came into my mind: *Becca, you should know by now that, of course, you can't control what's going to happen.* I sighed out loud. Accepting that fact still felt like a bitter pill to swallow, but there was a kind of freedom in it too.

True, I had no idea how things would go today. I hoped the exchange would be easy (my desire for things to be simple still hadn't changed), but I felt more confident that I wouldn't just bow down to him like I had done in the past.

Sometimes, as part of this journey, I faltered and found myself feeling angry or disappointed in myself for all the things that I could have done differently. Sometimes I wished I could go back and shake my younger self by the shoulders, and ask, "Why didn't you tell someone about your father? Or talk to anyone about what happened with your mom? You could have gotten help!" Or, "Why did you stay with Jason when he made you feel bad about yourself? Why didn't you listen to your gut and leave him after he made you feel like shit?"

But what I had discovered as I began to understand more and more about myself is that I had done what I thought was right in order to keep myself safe. I didn't need to be shamed or blamed for doing my best in shitty situations. I deserved my own admiration and appreciation and love. I deserved to be held, to be seen, to be heard. I had been through a lot. I was fucking *strong* and, after all the work I had done and the warrior-self I had rediscovered, I knew I could trust myself to handle this.

Jason and his parents had driven more than eight hours the day before, coming all the way from Brownsville, towing a U-Haul behind the truck. They would be here any minute. The plan was that he would give me a check for the money he owed me and then load up his stuff from the garage and leave. I had asked my mom and Darren to be at the house when Jason arrived, to act as moral support and witnesses. They showed up now, hugging me and offering encouragement. As we waited in the driveway, I could hear Bianca whining in the backyard. She wanted to be part of this, I could tell.

Moments later, Jason's truck rumbled down the street and parked in front of the side gate, next to the garage. Jason leaned his head out the window and called to Bianca in the high-pitched voice he had always reserved especially for her. "Hey there, Bianca!"

Bianca, who had been wagging her whole body seconds before, now flung herself against the side gate. She started barking like crazy, growling and snarling. She was totally pissed. The fence was bending under her weight and I started to feel nervous about what she would do if she managed to get out. I went around to the gate and caught hold of her collar, leading her through the backyard so I could take her inside the house. As I closed the door to her crate, she licked my hand. "Thank you, Bianca. Thank you, but I can't let you go through the fence." She looked up at me and we smiled at each other.

I opened the front door and stepped outside again. I saw that Jason and his parents had gotten out of the truck and were waiting for me in front of the garage door.

"So, where's my check?" I asked, ignoring the usual niceties.

Jason turned to his mom. "I'm really sorry, Becca," she said. "He couldn't get it before we left. We'll just load up his things and then he'll get the check to you on Monday."

I looked at Jason, but he had walked back to stand beside the truck, apparently letting his mom handle this. I shook my head, disgusted. "No," I said firmly. "That wasn't the deal."

She rolled her eyes. "C'mon, Becca. We drove all the way from Brownsville. I promise he'll get you the money. Just open the garage so we can get his stuff."

I could feel adrenaline begin pulsing through my body. "No!" My eyes swept across Jason and his parents. "This is *bullshit.*"

"Becca. Open the garage," his mom repeated.

"I said no!" I shouted. "Fuck you! I'm calling my lawyer." I flipped open my phone and found the number. Luckily, my attorney answered on a Saturday. I quickly summarized the problem, then handed my phone to Jason's mom so they could talk. From the look on his mom's face, I knew I had won. No way in hell was Jason getting away with this.

After another minute, his mom hung up the phone and returned it to me. Ignoring her, I stared straight at Jason. With steel in my voice, I declared, loud enough for even the neighbors to hear, "You will pay me and then you will get your stuff. Until then, I am not opening my garage."

Jason and his parents whispered together, gave me one last look, and then they all got back into the truck.

I was shaking as I watched them drive away. Darren and my mom walked with me back into the house, and I crumpled to the floor. It took me a minute to realize the cries I was hearing were mine because, really, I felt fantastic. Empowered. So strong.

Why was I crying?

Because that's what I did when my adrenaline needed a release. That's how I allowed myself to feel things. Crying wasn't a weakness. After decades of suppressing my body's wisdom, I was learning to lean into it and welcome these responses. I felt like Jason's visit had been a test of my resolve. It's so easy to be positive and strong when everything is hunky-dory, but when shit hits the fan, what do you do? Do you fall back into old habits and thought patterns? I didn't, not this time.

"Becca, I am so proud of you," my mom said, as she knelt next to me, rubbing my back.

I lifted my head and smiled at her. "I'm really proud of myself too!"

Darren reached out his hand and helped me stand up. The intensity of the last half hour had subsided with my tears and now I felt fucking amazing. "God, that felt good!" I said loudly, suddenly feeling pumped. "I mean, what a shit show, but . . . *aah!*" I couldn't contain my pride and excitement. I wanted to high five someone, scream in victory, throw a chair, *something.* I took a minute, then decided to call my attorney again.

"So, what do we do now?" I asked her.

"You wait until you get your money," she said. "It's that straightforward."

Hmm. I wished everything was that straightforward: *If you do this, then he'll do that.* But I knew it didn't always work that way. That had been the kind of promise I had lived by all my life, and it had taken my utter destruction for me to see that it was a false hope.

For too long, everything I did or said or believed had been dependent on someone else's behavior. I had become invisible, existing only in relation to them. Over time, that voice inside of me—that quiet defiance, the one who called bullshit and took a stand—had been growing and expanding, crowding out the other voices around me. At first, the force of that voice was so strong, it scared me. It was uncontrollable, unpredictable, assertive, demanding, and I wasn't sure I could trust it to keep me safe.

As a child, I had learned that it was safer to listen to what others were telling me. My life was easier when I accepted their truths as my own. Questioning and resisting only led to fear and anger and trouble. *My* voice was consistently silenced. I was shushed, dismissed, ignored, over and over. What I asked for didn't matter and sometimes, raising my voice made things worse. To stay safe, I had to effectively snuff out my flame.

But I wasn't scared of that voice anymore.

I knew, from burning those Disney pictures, that it could take a while to build a fire. The first match doesn't always light, the fuel doesn't always catch right away, and it's kind of startling when those sparks start popping and the heat burns your eyes. But if I wanted the flames to grow, wanted those embers to ignite, I had to keep coaxing those sparks and tossing things in to see what would light up. I knew I might be tempted to keep my fire small, because a small fire can be extinguished or controlled fairly easily. Letting it burn would mean others would see it. I would be exposed and vulnerable. That is the risk it takes to be bright and full and alive. I knew that as the flames began to roar higher, my first instinct would be to run and ask someone else for help. But how many times had I reached out for external reassurance? How many times had I listened to someone else tell me what was right or okay or acceptable? How many times had I let others dictate what I should do, how I should behave, or what I should believe?

Nah, enough of that bullshit, I thought, smiling to myself, feeling that defiant spark sizzling white-hot, burning inside of me.

Let's light this fucker up!

EPILOGUE

SUMMER 2023

A s I write this I am sitting out in the sun on our beautiful country property, with chickens announcing their eggs and the sound of our koi pond waterfalls in the background. My two boxer fur babies, Atlas and Zoe, rest in the sun near me, soaking up the rays while also being ready to protect their mama from a "mean ol' delivery person" at a moment's notice. My mind drifts off sometimes, thinking about what I'll make for dinner—maybe I'll create something new tonight! The world feels so ripe with possibility these days, but I'm still learning to embrace uncertainty and enjoy the journey. I still have my love notes, although they have evolved over time. I have consolidated them onto one page that I read to myself every morning with a smile on my face and my hand on my heart. I feel strong, empowered, and so proud of the woman I am and continue to become.

Darren is my partner in this wild and beautiful life we now share. We married in 2011 in a small ceremony on the beach with a group of family and friends by our side. I laugh now at all our conversations over the years as we've worked through differences and decisions, learning together to build trust and a strong foundation. As we built trust, I began to share all the remaining pieces of my past with him, knowing that sharing those darker corners of myself not only helped him understand me, but also helped me to continue to more deeply understand myself. We have grown individually and as a couple together over the years, and as we each continue to evolve, change, and grow, so too will our bond. We own several properties together that he manages, and we are also in the process of building and designing a boat together, which is the result of a plan we created in 2015 to travel around the world by sailboat. We want to explore and experience all this world has to offer on land, under water, among people and cultures, and in the remote corners where there is nothing but nature. The ocean is calling to us.

I remain separated from my father. It is one of the healthiest boundaries I've ever established. He still exists in this world, but he's not living rent free in my mind. I'm sure that he, and possibly others, see me as cold, unforgiving, or a bitch. If that happens because I am holding a boundary, respecting and honoring myself, then so be it. I know what is necessary for my health and well-being, and I will communicate that to others so my soul can shine bright and be in harmony with my body and mind. Sometimes that means putting myself first and not giving others what they want. Some may call that being a bitch. I call it being a badass.

My mom and I had a long journey in attempt to rebuild our relationship. We tried talking and connecting on a deeper level for several years, but eventually it became clear that the walls were too high, the damage too deep, the effort unbalanced and that letting her go was another necessary decision. Sometimes even if you want a relationship to work with your whole heart, it doesn't.

My sister is now married with two beautiful kiddos. She is an incredible cook and also works her medical magic in a neonatal intensive care unit. This year, we decided to make our relationship a priority and began getting together every month to catch up, support each other and share some laughs.

Aside from recounting the events of this book, I've rarely thought about Jason since the divorce. Because of the spousal immunity laws in Texas, I was not involved in the criminal proceedings, and I didn't follow anything about his situation back then. I simply did not want to know the details. I just wanted him out of my life. I do know that he pled guilty to indecency with a child by sexual contact and is living with the consequences that were issued. He eventually did hand over the money he owed me per the divorce decree, and I allowed him to get his things.

In the fall of 2009, I transferred to a different school to continue teaching. Stephanie and her daughter were part of the "Jason situation," and I wanted that as far from my thoughts as possible. I taught for eight years and then left teaching children in 2014 to begin teaching adult clients how to do mortgages.

At first I was so angry at Stephanie and her daughter for bringing everything to light and bringing charges against Jason, but now I am grateful for them. They stood up and said something, and helped ensure that other girls would not become victims too. It took them standing up and speaking out— starting a fire, so to speak—to bring about justice and change. At the time, I was so focused on my own pain and suffering that I didn't even think about what they must have been going through and continued to endure as the case against Jason progressed through the court system. I hope they have found peace, healing, and joy in their own lives.

———

Recently, I came across the term "betrayal blindness." Coined by Dr. Jennifer Freyd, betrayal blindness describes the experience of hiding information from oneself, or pretending not to see it, because the reality of the truth would threaten your relationships or sense of safety. The phrase almost perfectly describes what I experienced growing up. I understand, now, that shutting out or pretending not to see the reality of certain behaviors was a coping mechanism I used for my safety and well-being.

I'd long thought of myself as being a perfectionist and a "people pleaser" because those terms accurately described how I felt and acted as a young adult. But over time, I've come to see that for me, at the root of it all is a deep need to feel safe and loved. In order to feel that as I grew up, I needed to control things. If everything was in control or under my control, then I felt safe. If I was perfect at everything, with both the exterior and interior elements under control, then I felt loved. If I could make everyone happy—as in every single person whom I interacted with or that even knew I existed—if *they* liked me, then I was perfect and everything was under control and I felt safe and loved. The best way I knew to please others and get them to like me was to act happy and cheerful all the time. If I looked and seemed happy to everyone, they were pleased and I earned their approval. Having their approval helped me feel in control—and so the inward spiral of logic goes.

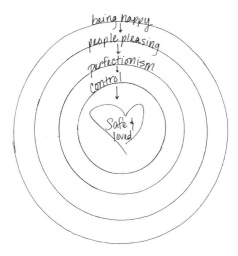

Recognizing these core needs, and the extent I went to try to meet those needs, I can now see my younger self, my motives, and my coping mechanisms with new clarity. I continue to dive deeper, asking myself new questions like: *Do I need these strategies to feel safe and loved? What benefits do I get from control? How does control work against me? Is there safety and love within myself without control?* This is my next step, my next edge to explore.

Because she knew I was writing this book, one day my mom sent me a picture of little four-year-old me, wearing a beautiful golden dress that my Grams had made, just like the one Belle wore in *Beauty and the Beast*. I held the photo in my hand and remembered screaming with glee as I took that dress out of the beautifully wrapped box. I immediately tore off my clothes, throwing them aside until I stood in nothing but my flower underpants, begging my mom to help me put the dress on.

As my mom and Grams draped the dress gently over me, I smiled the biggest smile and squealed with delight. "Mommy! I'm so pretty! I'm a princess!" She put on my favorite *Snow White* soundtrack and utter joy and freedom radiated out of me as I twirled across the carpet, lungs bursting with song, letting the music flow through me.

Back then, in those early childhood days, my innocent voice filled our home, floor to ceiling, reverberating around our two-story house. Eyes closed, face lifted, skirts swishing, and feet dancing, nothing else existed for me. I always wanted to hear myself over the soundtrack, so I sang as loudly as I could. Everyone knew what the princesses sounded like, but I wanted to know what *I* sounded like. I needed to hear the sound of my own voice.

As you now know, in the years that followed, I lost that strong sense of self; my voice was silenced; my innocence stolen from me.

After years of intense personal growth, in 2021 I had a zing of inspiration to take voice lessons. It was like my soul was asking for what it wanted, and I had been quiet enough to hear the request. I found an amazing coach and we started with sounds, single notes, ridiculous vocal noises, and purposefully sounding "bad." For the first several sessions, I sang a song I had chosen and then we talked about how it felt, what I noticed, and how I could tune into myself even more. My coach noticed that I was very good at imitating others' voices and asked why I thought that might be. The realization hit me like a Mack truck, and I started bawling my eyes out: "Because they are good at singing. They sound good and are successful and that is proof that they are good. If I sound like them, then I am good." As I continued to cry, I realized that I was still basing my value on the approval of others—*if I sing well, then I am worthy of love.*

My coach quietly spoke words of encouragement, reassuring me that this was what we were working on together—rediscovering what *Becca* sounds like.

Reclaiming my voice has taught me that whenever we share our stories, speak our truth out loud, and bear witness to our experiences, we not only confront those who want to silence us, but we hold out a light for others who have lost their way. The world can certainly use more beautiful, blazing souls, and I, for one, am going to keep shining bright and calling bullshit on anyone and anything that tries to tell me I am not enough.

ACKNOWLEDGMENTS

Darren—Thank you so much for seeing the spark within me as I was first seeing it within myself, for loving me fiercely, for living unapologetically, and for being my soul's complement in this life. We are not two halves that make a whole—we are two whole people that create magic. Blue paint and yellow paint—together making a vibrant green. I love you beyond words!

Grams—For most of my life, we lived far away, but you always dropped everything and came to help when I needed you most. Thank you for the incredibly special bond we share and for making me all those princess dresses so long ago. Love you bunches and bunches!

To my sister—Thank you so much for reviewing some of the book memories with me and helping me get a more full picture on some of the really hard ones. The memory of us holding each other on the sidewalk is seared into my mind—not because we were going through hell, but because we were connected together in sisterly love.

To my brother—My favorite memories are of us playing Mario Kart and Donkey Konga, all of my worries slipping away as I was spending time playing with you.

To my beta readers and friends—Melissa, Jaime, Candance, Christine, and Chris—y'all are the best! I cannot even begin to describe the terror of sending my first draft out to you for review, but you each gave me invaluable feedback that helped me continue to smooth out the kinks and buff until it shined. You held space for the sensitive nature of my story while still being honest about what you thought and where I could improve. Your words of encouragement and belief in me helped bolster me in times of doubt. Thank you from the bottom of my heart!

To Karen Holmes—I simply could not have written this book to the depth that it is written without you. Thank you for helping me pick through what I thought I wanted to write in order to find the book that wanted to be written. For your gentle compassion as we dove into traumatic and difficult memories and your tenacity to dig deeper even when you knew it may hurt, but there would be healing there as well. I am grateful beyond belief for you truly seeing me, both who I am now and my younger self. She wanted to speak, and you helped me find and bring forth her voice. I will forever cherish our time together!

There were endless amounts of people helping, so it's possible I might miss someone, but please know that all of you have a special place in my heart for your guidance, professionalism, encouragement and smiles:

Thanks to KT Leota-Khuong for helping me at the beginning of this project, and to Sophie May for taking over when needed to help guide me the rest of the way. You both were amazing cheerleaders and shepherds throughout the process! To Claire Brudner and Becca Kadison for your magical management of all the behind-the-scenes processes. To Rose Friel for your masterful matchmaking leading me to Karen. To Ami Hendrickson for your beautiful wordsmithing with my back cover copy and Jess LaGreca for your vision and design savvy in creating my striking cover and beautiful interior layout. To my editors Nikki Van Noy and Caroline Hough for double-checking all my work, Samantha Hendrix and Madelyn Lindquist for your proofreading prowess, and Monika Finn for your help evaluating my graphics. Finally, to Julie Scheife and Mayfly Design for helping me get to the publishing finish line.

Made in the USA
Coppell, TX
16 December 2023

25486389R00116